$200 VALUE for FREE!!*
FREE TWO WEEK TRIAL!*

TRY OUT TRENDFUND.COM FOR TWO WEEKS-FREE!
That's right, it's free with no obligations! Simply tear out this handy reminder, take it to your computer, log on and go to the following web site to sign up for your free two-week trial membership.

www.trendfund.com

See for yourself why Trendfund.com has grown by leaps and bounds. Meet Tiny in the chat room and follow his technical trades live as they are called. Get the latest on his charting techniques and Technical Analysis. Read Waxie's uncannily accurate daily thoughts about the market and follow his stock plays, plus his option and stock picks of the week. Or, if futures are your game, trade Teresa's futures calls. Though individual results vary, some trial members have made more than enough during the two-week free trial period to cover their membership costs for a year! Give it try! It's free for two weeks so you have nothing to lose! Below is just a sample of the extensive Trendfund membership benefits.

- ✓ Tiny's Technical Analysis, stock and options plays.
- ✓ Waxie's Trend Analysis, stock and option plays.
- ✓ Teresa's Futures Analysis, stock and futures plays.
- ✓ A live chat room for realtime stock, options, and futures calls.
- ✓ Weekly stock and options plays.
- ✓ Daily market commentary, projections, and news.
- ✓ An Alert Reporter for alerts and trades, virtually in realtime.
- ✓ Market Views for breaking market news, and more.
- ✓ Email alerts related to the market, IPOs, and other plays.
- ✓ Earnings calendars, and earnings season plays.
- ✓ Trend tracking and trend plays.
- ✓ Online chat room classes and other educational materials.
- ✓ Access to chat and class archives.
- ✓ And more...

** This offer applies to new clients only. Existing members, prior members, and prior trial members are excluded. Member benefits are subject to change.*

Charting

An Introduction To Technical Analysis And Its Concepts

By

Michael "Tiny" Saul

Charting

An Introduction To Technical Analysis And Its Concepts

Copyright © 2003, Trend Fund Corp.
All rights reserved!

Printed in the United States of America.
First Printing: July 2003
Published by Trendfund Corp.
www.trendfund.com

ALL RIGHTS RESERVED!

This book, nor any portion thereof, may not be stored in a retrieval system, transmitted, scanned, or otherwise copied or reproduced by any means in any form without prior written permission from publisher.

EXAMPLES AND ILLUSTRATIONS

The examples and illustrations provided in this book are for illustration purposes only. Stock prices reflect the prices at the time of publication, or in some cases, may have been fabricated to better illustrate the concepts being presented. Similarly, stock or company names were chosen arbitrarily for illustration purposes only. The concepts presented could just as easily apply to any stock.

TRADEMARKS

To the extent applicable, products, services, names, and other content contained in this book are trademarks or registered trademarks of their respective holders and companies.

LIMITS OF LIABILITY AND WARRANTY DISCLAIMER

Author and publisher make no warranty of any kind, expressed or implied, regarding the information contained in this book, and shall not be liable in any event for incidental or consequential damages in connection with, or arising out of, the furnishing or usage of information contained herein.

Dedication

This book is dedicated to the memory of my mother, whose devotion to teaching, love and support made me the man I am today.

Acknowledgements

I would like to thank the following people who made this book possible:

Rodger Smith for all of his help in the production of this book.

Michael "WAXIE" Parness for the opportunity...I'm grateful for all your help and hope that I can reciprocate some day.

My wife Janine for her support, not only with help in editing this book, but in life.

My father for all of his encouragement through the good times and the bad, and for always believing I would be a success.

All of the staff at Trendfund.com for making my work environment the best there is.

All of the members at Trendfund.com who inspired me to get this book done as soon as possible (four years ain't bad, is it?).

And Stitchel Frangen, who's assistance, dedication and humor have also been a big help through the tough times.

About The Author

Michael "Tiny" Saul became Trendfund.com's Chief Technical Analyst (CTA) in 1999. Armed with an in-depth knowledge of the stock market, trading, and Technical Analysis, plus years of hands-on experience, Tiny has guided thousands of Trend Traders through the rigors of trading both Bull and Bear markets.

Tiny's unique blend of education, humor and insight has helped grow Trendfund.com's member base over 1000% since inception. He has lectured at over ten Trend Trading Seminars (with more on the way), and he is also featured in the "Trend Trading To Win" video series.

Tiny lives in New Jersey with his wife Janine. Their two cats, PrincessKitty and Buster are currently at Tiny's father's house, on an extended vacation. In his spare time, Tiny enjoys trying to avoid exercise and what else, looking at charts!

Table Of Contents

Foreword

In the middle of 1999 both Michael "Tiny" Saul and I were members of another online chat room (that shall go nameless!). I was making money and doing very well on my own through what we now call Trend Trading, but people in that room kept talking about this thing called Technical Analysis, or Charting. I had heard about this concept and given that I was, and still am, always looking for an "edge", it seemed intriguing to me. I asked someone in the room, who had befriended me, what I could do to learn about Technical Analysis and he steered me toward, well, TINY.

I remember feeling a little weirded out by the fact that upon my very first contact with Tiny, he gave me his home phone number and told me he'd be happy to help me. Being a good New Yorker, I'm always a little skeptical when someone I've never met offers to help me and gives me their home number the very first time I have contact with them! New York isn't Kansas, after all, ya know!

But, since I was hungry to learn about Technical Analysis, I called Tiny. The first conversation we had lasted, from what I recall, several hours. He was honest, open, informative and VERY funny. Based on our phone call, I had this picture of a guy in my head that was either a body builder or a midget. I decided he was a body builder. I was wrong on both counts.

However, I wasn't wrong to think that this was a genuine, kind, funny, and profoundly interested in helping others person. And, maybe most of all, he was extremely passionate about Technical Analysis! He seemed to know EVERYTHING! And, even better, he was interested in learning MORE and helping others, just like I was.

I think it was our third conversation where I told him a little about myself and that I was thinking about starting my own website to help other traders make money and be successful. He said that was great but I think he was probably thinking to himself, "oh boy, another big shot wannabe!".

Shortly thereafter, I asked Tiny to be my CTA (Chief Technical Analyst) of what would eventually become Trendfund.com. He said that he was interested, but then I told him that he wouldn't be paid for a while. He said that he had to think about it. I told him to watch my calls and decide what he wanted to do. He'll tell you how amazed he was that I was actually legit.

My jaw drops every time I see Tiny do a seminar, or listen in on an online class. He is a true teacher and believer in what he does, and the good it can do for others.

When WE started Trendfund.com the idea was to create a community for traders that was safe from the investing community and the media's ideas of what was right about the market. Given my scattered family background, in hindsight I think I wanted to create a new extended family of traders, all looking to help each other make money, and be successful in other areas of their lives. Tiny has been possibly THE driving force for the success of Trendfund.com outside myself. His passion empowers 1000s of others to seek their own dreams and achieve their own successes.

When I asked Tiny to work with me for nothing, I promised him that one day he'd make a lot of money with Trendfund.com. All I asked of him was for him to remain passionate and loyal to our members, and to put their needs as equal to his own. Tiny has kept that promise to me, and I've kept my promise to him. He's helped grow Trendfund.com from a tiny trading community into the true leader in alternative investing. I'm profoundly grateful that I happened upon Tiny from the other chat room.

Like everything else in life, I believe there are no coincidences. I'm glad that I made that first phone call and didn't let my imagination run wild. Tiny is one of the good guys and I am proud to be a part of Tiny's first book! I congratulate my partner and my very good friend, Tiny, and wish him continued success - no one deserves it more than he!

Whether you are a total newbie (new to Technical Analysis), and don't know a head and shoulders from a tongue in cheek, or you are a wise old "chartist", I believe this book will provide you with not only the foundation to begin your wonderful journey as a trader (or investor), but the power to enact it for PROFITS!

Enjoy his book and tell him about it, cause it'll give him a big smile.

Michael Parness
CEO Trendfund.com
CEO Trend Trading to Win

1 - Introduction

Welcome to "Charting", a practical guide to charts and technical analysis.

Charting contains a wealth of information about charts and trading stocks that you can readily adapt to your own situation.

This book discusses many strategies that are applicable to daytrading, swing trading, and to intermediate or long term investing as well. Whether you are just starting out in the stock market, are an experienced trader, or are an investor, you'll gain valuable insights into technical analysis and using charts.

If you are new to charting, you'll find the information you need to get up to speed quickly. Page-by-page, you will learn more about charts and how to use them. To build a foundation from which to begin, there is a brief history of technical analysis and general chart descriptions. Then you can proceed through progressively more advanced charting concepts at a pace that is comfortable for you.

Each topic comes with fully illustrated examples. And many of the examples include specific trading suggestions. Plus, walkthroughs of the whole process, from the analysis to the trade, are provided at the end of the book to help reinforce what you've learned.

Among numerous other topics, you'll learn ways to time the entries and exits of trades, which for many traders is one of the most difficult skills to master. And yet, it is a crucial skill that must be mastered in order to profit consistently. The information contained in this book is intended to help you achieve that goal, and more.

Following is a sample of the topics you'll find in the pages ahead:

- Price and Dot To Close charts
- Line charts, HLC & OHLC charts
- Bar charts, Japanese Candlestick charts
- Swing Point Highs and Swing Point Lows
- Directional Trends & Trading Ranges
- Trendlines & Accelerating Trendlines
- Support and Resistance
- Patterns such as Pennants, Flags, and others
- Moving Averages
- Breakouts, Breakdowns, and Trend Reversals
- Technical Indicators
- Momentum, Volume, and Impulses
- Accumulation and Distribution
- Fibonacci Analysis
- Analysis and trading suggestions
- More...

How To Use This Book

Many of the charting concepts build upon information provided earlier. For that reason, I recommend that you work your way through the book sequentially from the beginning to the end.

Also, many trading suggestions and examples are interspersed throughout the book, so skipping around could cause you to miss a potentially profitable trading tidbit.

As you read through the book, you might find it useful to use your own charting software or an online charting service for additional study and reinforcement of the discussed topics.

Finally, as is the case with a single reading of any new subject, a second reading could provide an even deeper understanding. Once you are finished, you will hopefully find the book to be a worthwhile resource for future reference whenever the need arises.

Now, let's get started!

What is technical analysis?

Technical analysis is a method of using charts, graphs, and market data to evaluate individual stocks or the overall market. Current and historical patterns and trends are analyzed to help predict future prices and trends.

Here are examples of how you can use technical analysis:

- To select stocks to buy, sell or sell short
- To time the overall market or individual stocks
- To analyze entry and exit points
- To study stock and market trends
- To study a stock's price movement over time
- To predict future price performance
- To determine support and resistance levels
- And more...

The main tools of technical analysis are price charts. Most charts cover a stock's price movement over a set period of time. However, there are exceptions such as the *point and figure* chart and other charts that only study price and don't take time into account. Point and figure charting is not a technique I prefer so I won't be discussing it in this book. However, I will be describing a variety of other charts.

You can use technical analysis to select among stocks or indexes, and to time entry and exit points for trades. You can also use it to keep you out of a potentially bad position. For example, you may be about to enter a long or short position based on other factors and discover the charts are telling you "no" or "not yet". This is what makes Technical analysis a very powerful tool. If you are interested in getting the most out of your trading or investing, I strongly encourage you to learn all you can about it.

Fundamental Analysis

Technical analysis differs significantly from fundamental analysis, which often measures a stock against intangibles such as future earnings, financial "value", P/E ratios, and other barometers you may or may not have heard of. Since the goal of any trader or investor is to more accurately time the entries and exits of trades, using fundamental analysis is problematic because it is based partially on intangible data.

For example, a company might project a certain amount in earnings for an upcoming quarter only to make an unexpected announcement a month or so later stating earnings are coming in below the prior estimates. If you had bought the stock based on their previous earnings estimate (or even their actual earnings report), you would likely have taken a hit when the revised earnings projections were announced.

Since fundamental analysis uses intangibles, such as future earnings estimates, it's unreliable for the purpose of timing entries and exits.

Technical analysis measures a stock or the market against tangibles such as its past stock price, or its parent index. It uses past tangible market data to help predict future price performance.

Just keep in mind that you can use either fundamental or technical analysis to decide what stock to trade, but only technical analysis can tell you when to enter and exit a trade.

Forefathers Of Technical Analysis

This section provides a brief historical overview of technical analysis. As you might imagine, the individuals introduced here did far more than can be discussed in this brief introduction. If you desire to know more about them, there are many other books available that focus specifically on their theories.

Charles Dow

Charles Dow is considered the grandfather of technical analysis. Even though Japanese Candlesticks were being used as far back as the 1100's, Charles Dow is thought of as the inventor of Western technical analysis. He essentially laid the groundwork for all technical analysis that has followed. Additionally, he was the first editor of the *Wall Street Journal* ®, and he came up with a variety of technical analysis theories.

My personal opinion is that some of his approaches to technical analysis are very useful, while others need to be modified and brought up to date.

For example, the Dow theory uses closing prices only and does not use highs, lows, or opening prices. The charting examples provided later show other approaches that offer more flexibility and as a result, are more useful in today's market.

Additionally, Charles Dow's approach compares the Dow Industrials to the Transports and Utilities Averages, and looks for convergence or divergence (whether they move toward each other, together, or apart from one another). Since the Transports, which include railways, planes, trucking companies, etc., are no longer the market driving force they once were, the value of their role in technical analysis has diminished. Instead of using the Transports, comparing today's major indices to each other can be very useful and it is a good way to use the

Charles Dow theory. For example, you can compare the Dow Industrials with the Nasdaq, or the S&P 500 with the NY composite. The S&P 500, the "big cap" benchmark, is a nice broad measure of the markets, while the Nasdaq is a good measure of the technology markets. It's often helpful to see how the broad market (which includes technology stocks) is moving in relation to just the technology stocks.

One of Charles Dow's approaches that I do feel is applicable describes how the market moves in "up legs" and "down legs", which consists of three types of movement: primary, secondary, and minor. The primary move is the main directional trend, or movement, of the market. The secondary move is a reactive, countertrend move, and the minor moves are the small day-to-day fluctuations.

Richard Schabacker

Schabacker expanded upon Charles Dow's work. He formulated theories for gaps and classified common "patterns", which are repeating formations that occur on charts. He also used trendlines and 'support and resistance' levels. Both are extremely important for modern technical analysis.

Schabacker came up with great advice about tape action (or flow of the market's action). A paraphrase of what he said follows:

If the market does not do what your primary analysis says it should, it's time to change your analysis and cut your losses short.

This is a key trading rule. If your analysis causes you to think the market will go up, but it doesn't go up, then you are wrong! It's not the market that is wrong. Don't hold onto your position refusing to believe that your analysis is wrong. Accept the fact that you are wrong, take your losses and get out of your position before small losses become large losses. To put it simply, don't fight the market.

Richard Wycoff

Richard Wycoff introduced the concept of volume, the quantity of shares trading hands, to analyze accumulation and distribution. He also introduced the idea of buying and selling climaxes. A buying climax occurs when a stock has one last big push up, usually accompanied by a surge in volume. Afterwards, both the volume and price begin to fall. Since all of the buyers are now in the stock, there is no one left to support a further price advance. The opposite occurs with selling climaxes, where anxious sellers "capitulate", or throw in the towel and give up on the market. This is often when the best long trades are made.

Ralph Elliot

Ralph Elliot introduced the famous Elliot Wave theory. He came up with the idea that the market unfolded in a series of waves. The Elliot Wave theory is similar to the Charles Dow theory, except where the Dow theory has three waves; the Elliot Wave theory has five.

Elliot Wave theory is based on the theory that the market moves in five primary waves when it is an impulsive move (a strong forceful move). For example, when the market has an impulsive move up, it moves in five waves then when it corrects, it moves down in three waves. Of course, the opposite is the case when the primary impulsive move is to the downside rather than the upside.

Individual opinions vary regarding the usefulness of the Elliot Wave theory. Some traders like it, while others don't. An in-depth discussion of Elliot Wave theory is beyond the scope of this book but if you are interested in exploring it further, there are many books that specialize on Elliot Wave theory. Other modern-day Elliot Wave theorists you might consider checking into include Hocberg, Miner, Prechter, and Frost.

W.D. Gann

Gann is a popular technical analysis pioneer. He believes that *time and price* are important elements in timing the market, and that time should be taken into consideration during market moves. That is, if the market moves in a certain direction for a certain period of time, the time-length of the move is an indicator of whether it is likely to continue or reverse.

Gann also worked on other more esoteric theories such as how astrology and geometry affected the markets, which are once again beyond the scope of this book.

2 - Price Charts

As previously mentioned, the main tools of technical analysis are price charts. Depending on the charting software you use, a variety of options are typically available for customizing charts according to your own preferences. You can choose among options such as:

- Price display options - HLC, OHLC, Bar, Dot, Close, Candlestick, etc.
- Technical indicators -Volume, Stochastics, RSI, MACD, etc.
- Time frames / periods - intraday, daily, weekly, monthly, etc.
- Time frequencies / intervals - 1 min, 5 min, hourly, daily, weekly, etc.
- Comparisons - other stocks, indexes, etc.
- Overlays - moving averages (MA), Simple MA, Exponential MA, etc.

Since the specifics for how to display a particular chart varies widely and the instructions are provided with your preferred charting software, this book doesn't try cover all of the possible variations. Though the book touches on a variety of charts, the main focus is on the type of charts and display options that I've found to be most useful for general technical analysis, analyzing trends, selecting stocks, timing entries and exits, and managing other aspects of trades. Most of the information can be applied to any trading style, whether it's daytrading, swing trading, or long term investing.

Price charts plot prices at a specified frequency (or interval) for a specified timeframe (or time period). The terms *frequency* and *interval* are often used interchangeably. Price charts come in a variety of styles such as Dot, Line, HLC, OHLC, and Japanese Candlesticks. A general description of these follows. Later, the "Chart Patterns" chapter provides more detailed information about chart pattern formations.

Dot Chart (Dot-On-Close)

The Dot Chart uses dots to plot closing prices for a specified frequency over a specified timeframe. Each dot reflects the closing price for the specified frequency. For example, if you display a chart with a 5-minute frequency, each dot reflects the closing price of one 5-minute time period. For a chart with a daily frequency, each dot reflects the closing price for a day, and so on. The following illustration shows a Dot Chart.

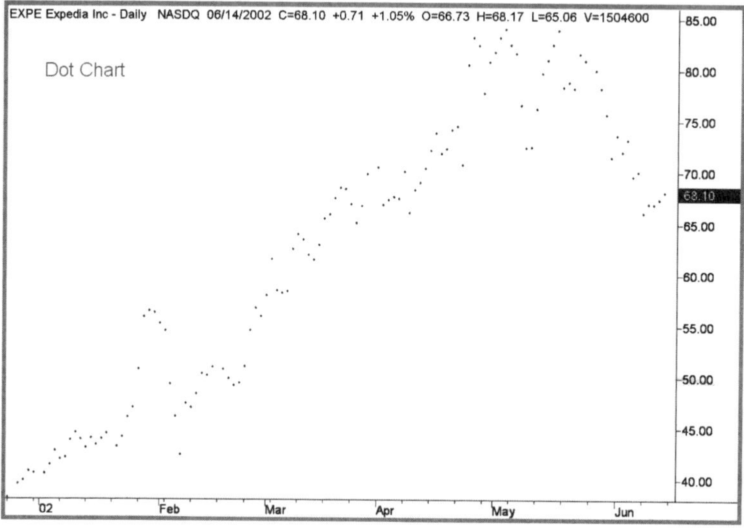

According to the Charles Dow theory, closing prices are all you need to perform an analysis; however, in my opinion, you really need more. The reason will become more apparent as other charts are described.

Line Chart

A Line Chart essentially connects the dots that were shown previously on the Dot Chart.

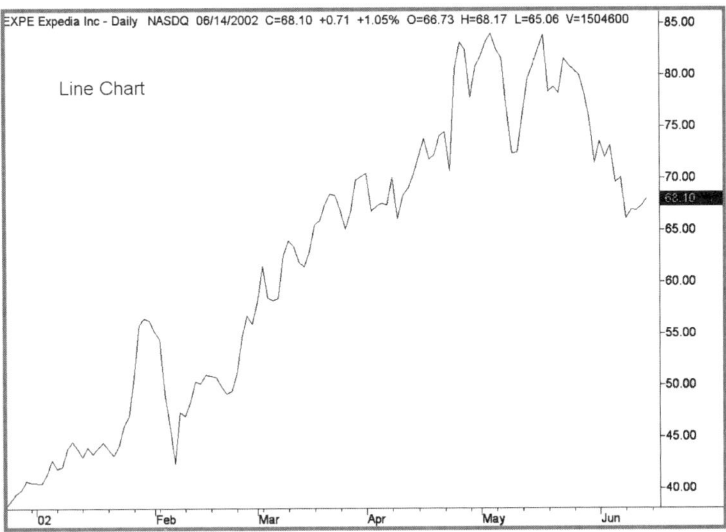

Like the Dot Chart, Line Charts are based on closing prices. While I occasionally use a Line Chart, I prefer other charts that show more information (these are explained soon). Still, Line Charts are the preferred choice of some traders.

HLC Chart (High-Lo-Close)

Although the HLC Chart, which is also called a Bar Chart, shows more than only the closing price (as opposed to the previously described Dot and Line Charts), I don't see any particular reason to use it. Another chart, the OHLC Chart (shown next), shows even more information. The HLC Chart shows the high, low, and closing prices. The OHLC Chart shows those and the opening prices as well.

Here is an example of the HLC Chart.

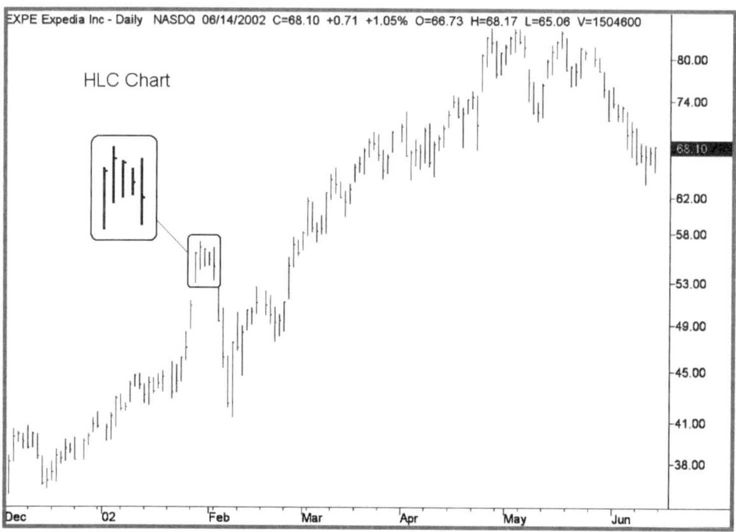

Please see the following "OHLC Chart" section for a more detailed explanation that also applies to the HLC Chart bars.

OHLC Chart (Open-Hi-Lo-Close)

As with the HLC Chart, the OHLC Chart is another form of a Bar Chart. This is my preferred choice for Bar Charts. Each bar shows prices for the open, high, low, and close for the time frequency period (e.g., 5-minute, hourly, daily, etc., depending on what you specified for the chart). So, all of the information that is needed to quickly see the price action for a bar's time period is contained right on the bar, which is an important consideration. Refer to the following sample OHLC Chart.

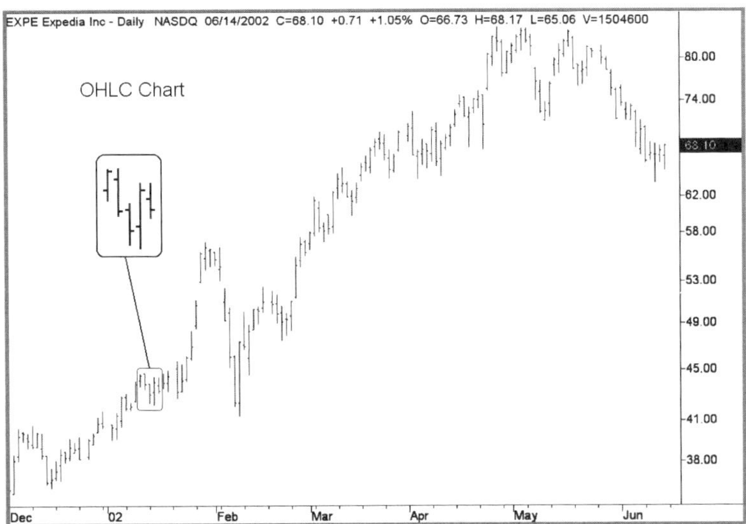

If you examine the bars on an OHLC Chart closely, you'll notice that they have small nubs on each side (see the following close-up view of a bar).

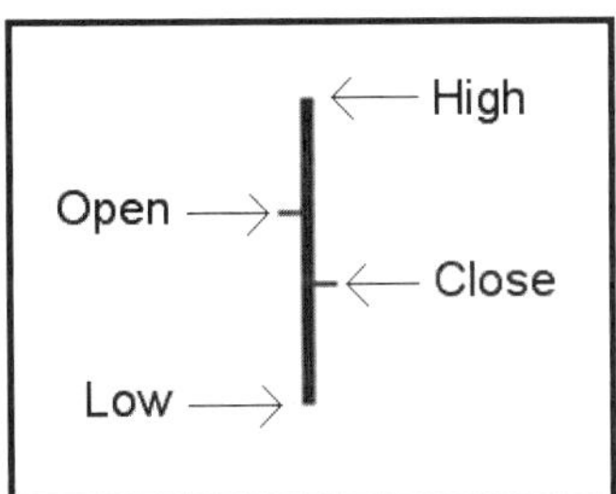

The nub on the left side of a bar is the opening price for the bar's time period. The nub on the right side of a bar is the closing price for the period. The top of the bar is the high price for the period, and the bottom of the bar is the low price.

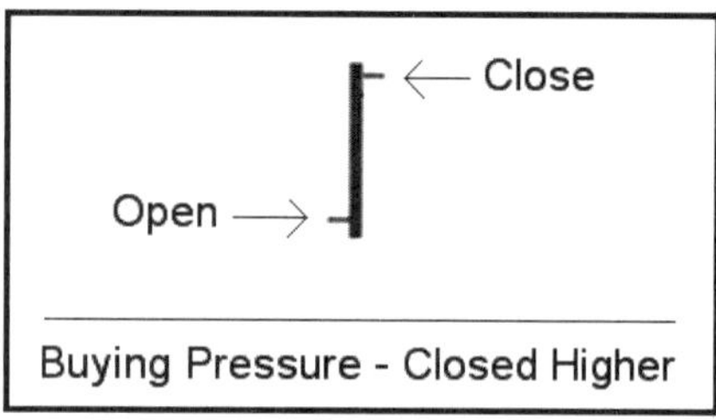

The position of a nub on the bar also communicates important information as well. If the nub that is located on the right side of a bar is higher than the nub on the left, it indicates there was more buying pressure than selling pressure going on during the period, since the closing price was higher than the opening price. If the nub on the right is at or near the top of a bar (i.e., it closes at its highs), there was buying into the close of the time period, which is a bullish indicator.

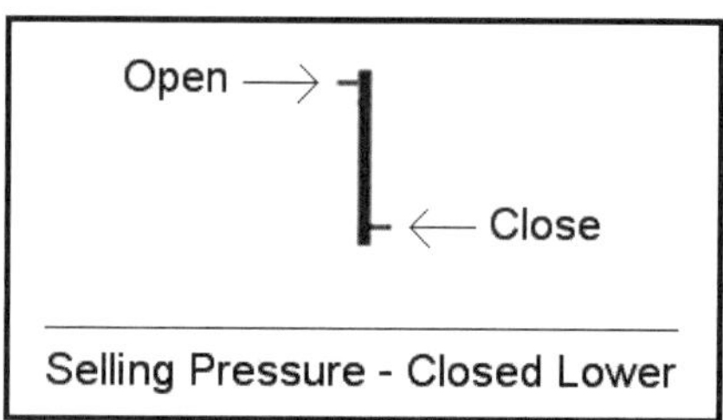

Conversely, the opposite is true if the closing price is lower than the opening price. If it closes at or near its lows, it indicates there was selling into the close, which is bearish.

When the price closes near the middle of the range, it indicates there was indecision during the period. In this case, you can check the next bar to determine whether the price action is bullish or bearish.

As you can see, the OHLC Chart shows everything you need, which is why this is my preferred choice for Bar Charts. While I frequently use OHLC charts, I also use Japanese Candlestick Charts and feel they are an even better choice. Since Candlestick Charts are color coded, you can see all of the preceding information easier and quicker (you don't need to look for small nubs). I encourage you to at least give them a try then you can choose according to your own preferences. Japanese Candlestick Charts are described next.

Japanese Candlestick Charts

Japanese Candlestick Charts date back to the 1100's, where they were used to trade rice contracts. These charts provide a wealth of information just by looking at the candle colors, shapes, and sizes.

Steve Nison is credited for bridging the Eastern and Western technical analysis gap by introducing Candlestick Charts to the United States. Their use and popularity have caught on like wildfire, and for good reason, as you'll soon see.

An example of a Japanese Candlestick Chart follows.

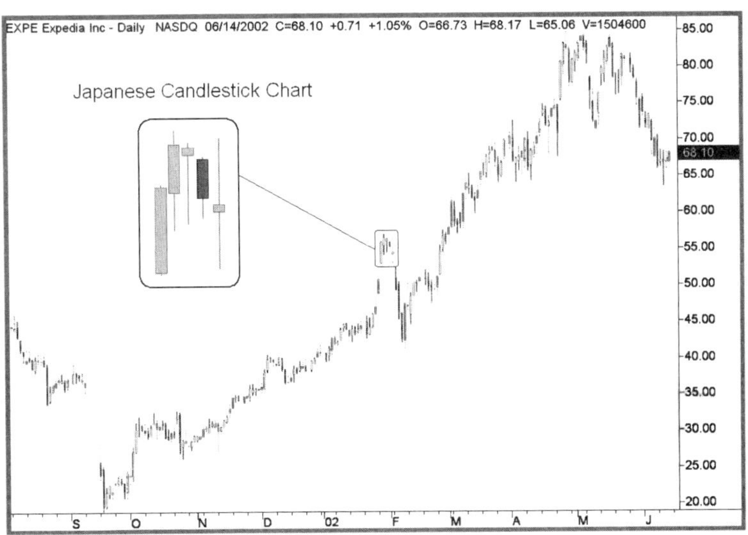

Following is a close-up view of candles.

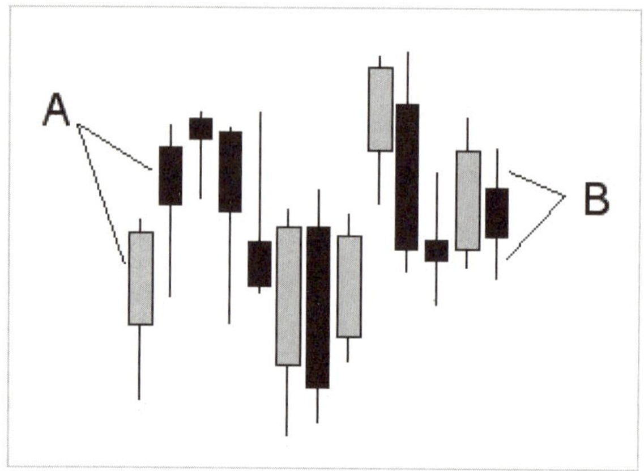

Each bar on the preceding chart is a candle. Candle appearances vary in many subtle but very important ways. Notice the difference in color, height, and the thin lines that extend above and below the thick part of the candles. All of these communicate important information.

Following is a general explanation of candlestick charts. A detailed explanation of individual candle variations comes later under "Candlestick Patterns" in the "Chart Patterns" chapter.

Although candle appearances vary, there are two primary types of candles: white (or light) candles and dark candles. The actual colors may differ depending on the charting software used, but I prefer to use green for white candles and red for dark candles.

The thick part of the candle is known as the real body (see A on the preceding illustration). The real body shows the opening and closing prices for a candle's time period. If the real body is white, the opening price is the bottom of the real body and the closing price is the top. If the real body is dark, the reverse is true. The opening price is the top of the real body and the closing price is the bottom. This gives us a quick view of who won the battle, the bulls by closing the stock higher than it opened, or the bears by closing the stock lower than it opened. Unlike bar charts, there is no searching for nubs; you only need to recognize colors when using Japanese Candlestick charts.

Referring to B in the preceding illustration, the thin lines extending from the top and/or bottom of the real body are called wicks, tails, or shadows. All of these terms can be used interchangeably.

The top of a candle, including the shadow, is the high price for the candle's time period. The bottom of the candle, including the shadow, is the low price.

You can use Candlestick Charts for any frequency (or time interval) such as 1-minute, 3-minute, 5-minute, daily, weekly, or monthly charts. They hold the pattern for any timeframe. Each candle corresponds to one interval of the specified time period.

It's easy to see why Candlestick Charts are so convenient to use. At a glance, you can see price highs, lows, opens, closes, and by its color, whether there was buying or selling pressure at the close of the candle's time period.

Although I occasionally go back to the basics and use OHLC Charts, I use Japanese Candlestick Charts the most, as they are my favorite type of chart. I strongly encourage you to use them as well, especially if you are just starting out. As you can see, they are very easy to learn.

As previously mentioned, the "Chart Patterns" chapter contains more specific information about candle patterns, including the large variety of individual candle shapes that are also important to take into consideration.

Bar Chart

Both HLC Charts and OHLC Charts are also referred to as Bar Charts. Please refer to the preceding descriptions, "HLC Chart" and "OHLC Chart", for information applicable to Bar Charts.

3 - Ranges And Trends

The general direction of a stock's price movement over a period of time is called a *trend*. If the price is moving up over time, then it is in an *uptrend*. If it is moving down, then it is in a *downtrend*. And, if the price is essentially moving sideways, it is said to be in a *range*, or *range bound*. These topics are explained in more detail in the pages that follow.

The Trend Is Your Friend

Where technical analysis is concerned, the old adage, *the trend is your friend*, couldn't be more true. One of the main principles of price action (or change) is that a trend has a much greater likelihood of continuing than reversing.

So, if the market is in an uptrend, overall, there's a much greater chance that it will continue to move higher rather than move lower. This is referred to as *trend persistence*. The same is true for a downtrend or a range bound market. Although a directional up- or down-trending market will eventually lead to a range bound market, and a range bound market will eventually lead to a directional trending market, you can't always predict the precise timing of the change. So, the goal is to recognize the current trend and use an applicable trading strategy (see "Trend Relativity" later in this chapter for more about this).

If you are in an uptrend, look to buy the price pullbacks. If you are in a downtrend, look to sell the rallies. In a range bound market, look to buy the low end of the range and sell the high end of the range. And while you can trade either, it's better to trade a directional trending market, since the moves tend to be larger. To illustrate this, see the following example.

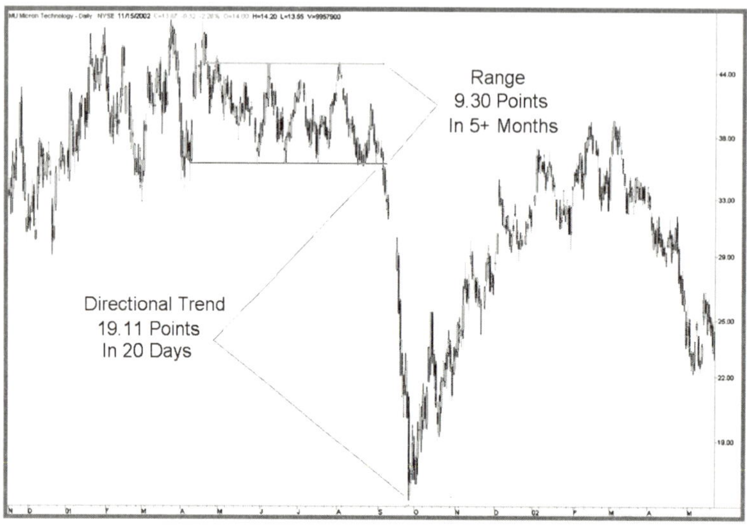

Notice that for 5-1/2 months the stock was stuck in about a 9.30-point range. However, when the stock broke out of the range and started a directional phase, it moved 19.11 points in only 20 days. The stock moved over twice as far in a fifth of the time during the directional trend. This example demonstrates the importance of keeping the following statistics in mind.

- 70% of the market's moves occur in only 20% of the time.
- The market tends to stay range bound 80-85% of the time.
- The market tends to move directionally 15-20% of the time.

The preceding is true for both long-term trends and for intraday trends.

On the preceding intraday chart, compare the length of the moves during the directional trends to that of the range bound phase.

The stock moved 2.37 points during the first directional downtrend, and then it was range bound for 4-5 hours. During that time, it only moved in a range of about .82, which would obviously be much harder to trade. You would more than likely have a tougher time attempting to scalp the .82 range, since you would have to pick near-perfect tops and bottoms to make good money. If you were a little off, you would most likely lose money. By contrast, in the directional phases the stock moved 2 or 3 times as much in about 1/5 the time. You can be less precise on your entries and exits, and still make money on a trade.

Once again, it illustrates the advantages of trading directional moves over a range bound market, whether trading intraday or a longer time period. It is possible to trade a range bound market, if the range is wide enough, but if not, it's best to stay out and wait for a directional move. Though it may test your patience, it pays to wait. A directional move will eventually come.

Swing Points And Trends

Charts are used to identify trends. In order to determine a trend, you need to identify the *swing points*. A *swing poin*t is the pivot point of the price, that is, the point where the price reverses direction.

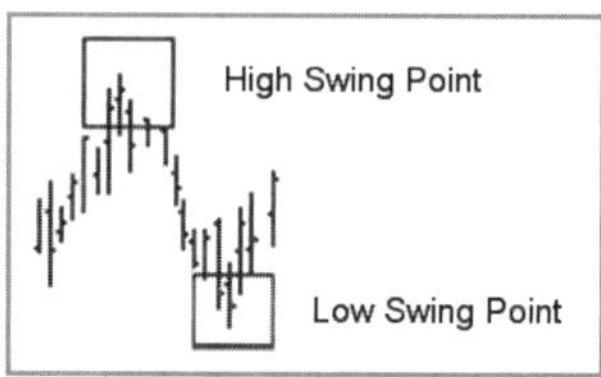

Referring to the preceding bar chart excerpt, notice that a *high swing point* is a high surrounded by two lower highs. And a *low swing point* is a low surrounded by two higher lows.

Uptrend

As seen in the following illustration, an uptrend is comprised of a series of higher *swing point highs*, and higher *swing point lows*.

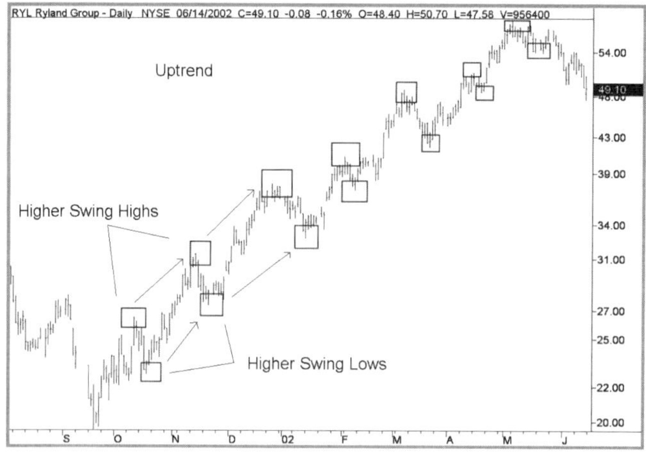

Downtrend

The next illustration shows that a downtrend is comprised of a series of lower swing point highs, and lower swing point lows. (You can also use the terms swing highs and swing lows for short.)

Ranges And Directional Trends

A range bound trend occurs when a stock or the market cycles back and forth in a range that is comprised of similarly priced swing highs and similarly priced swing lows over a period of time.

The following chart shows directional trends and ranges. Notice on the chart that a directional downtrend changes into a sideways range bound trend.

Trendlines

Trends are measured using trendlines. A trendline is drawn along three or more swing point highs or swing point lows.

The preceding illustration shows a downtrend line. Just remember that the trendline needs to touch at least 3 swing point highs to be valid. The next illustration shows an uptrend line.

You need 3 or more swing point lows to have a valid uptrend line.

Log & Linear Scales

Log charts price the chart graph using percentage moves. As a result, a 50% move on the chart will have the same 50% spacing between each subsequent move.

Linear charts show equal distances between each move. For example, if the spacing distance is 20 points, the spacing will be the same from 20 to 40, 40 to 60, and so on (see the following illustration).

Which chart is best mainly depends on the length of the time period and your own preferences. Notice that trendlines are drawn differently from one scale to the other, which is why I like to look at both scales when doing my analysis.

Generally, I prefer to use Log charts for longer-term views, and Linear charts for shorter-term views. When you are unsure about which to use, you can check them both and compare the results.

Accelerating Trendlines

An accelerating trendline occurs when each successive 3 points for which a trendline is charted results in a sharper sloping trendline than the preceding trendline. See the following illustration.

Accelerating trends can occur in both down trending and up trending markets. When you encounter accelerating trendlines, it indicates the trend is getting stronger.

Swing Lengths

Trends move in two directions, *impulsive* and *corrective*. There is an initial strong impulsive move, or primary move, followed by a less powerful corrective, or reactive move.

As previously explained, swing highs and swing lows are used to draw trendlines and determine trends. When analyzing trends, the length of the swing is also important. As long as the reaction of a swing in one direction does not exceed the preceding primary (or impulsive) swing, the trend is still intact. For an example of this, refer to the following illustration and explanation.

Notice the length of the swing between points 1 and 2, then compare it to the length of the following corrective swing between points 2 and 3. Since the second swing does not surpass the length of the first, and the move subsequently continues down, the downtrend remains intact.

Examining the previous illustration further, swing 4 to Z does not exceed the prior swing high, so the trend still remains intact. However, notice swing Z to A does not make a lower swing point low. And the next swing after that, the swing from points A to B, makes a higher swing high (higher than Z to A). Still, because the A to B swing does not take out the primary impulsive swing high at points 2 to 3, it did not technically break the downtrend. Instead, it simply took out a corrective swing high from points 4 to Z.

As long as the impulsive highs and lows are not taken out, the trend is still intact. Now, refer to the next illustration, which shows a change of trend more clearly.

Notice that the impulsive swing from point 2 to 3 makes a higher high, and is a greater length than the preceding swing down from 1 to 2. This indicates a change of trend.

As long as a downtrend is intact, you want to be ready to sell short every rally (you would sell short immediately following confirmation of each swing high point of the downtrend in the preceding example). Once the trend is broken, for example, after the impulsive swing from points 2 to 3 in the illustration, you want to get ready to buy the pullbacks. Particularly, the first pullback since the first corrective swing tends to be a strong, high percentage play. More specific examples of how to time entries for these types of trades are provided later.

Trading Trends And Ranges

Trend Relativity

The relationship between trends that are shown in two charts with different timeframes (e.g., hourly versus daily, etc.) is referred to as *trend relativity*. It's important not to mix timeframes from different charts when determining entry and exit points for a trade or you could inadvertently introduce trend relativity errors. For example, you wouldn't want to use the trends of an hourly chart to plan your entry for a trade, and those of a daily chart to exit the trade.

Refer to the following illustration. You'll see an hourly, daily, and weekly chart of the same stock and time period displayed side-by-side.

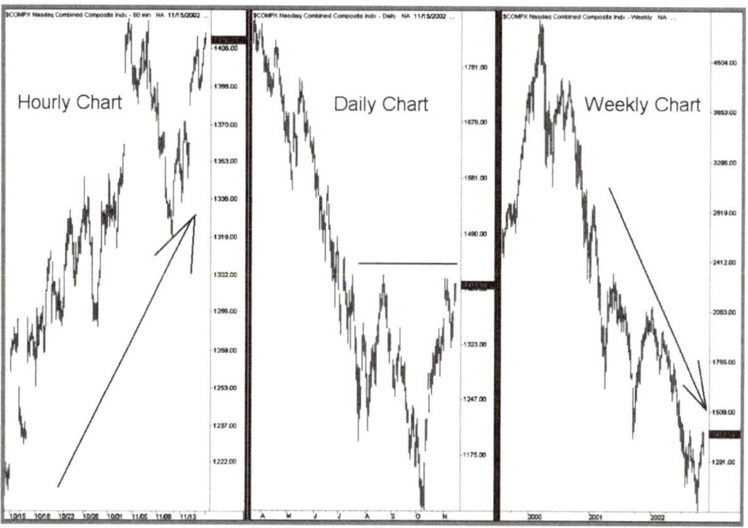

If you were trading based on the hourly chart (left), you are clearly in an uptrend. However, if you switch to a daily chart (center), you'll discover you are no longer in an uptrend. Instead, you are now in a range. In this case, you would want to be more careful about buying. Finally, the weekly chart shows that the market overall is actually in a downtrend. Here, you would want to be shorting the market, rather than buying. How the time period affects the trends between these different charts demonstrates the importance of paying attention to trend relativity.

While it's desirable to look ahead one time period to track overall trends, it's important that you don't inadvertently mix the two when entering and exiting your trades.

Chart Timeframe Suggestions

Here are a few suggestions for charts you might consider using based on your trading style:

Scalping: 1-minute and 5-minute (to look ahead)
Daytrading: 5-minute and hourly
Swing trading: hourly and daily
Intermediate trading: daily and weekly
Investing: weekly and monthly

Trading Tips For Trends And Ranges

Before making a trade, it's very important to know the trend of the market overall, and the trend of the stock you intend to trade. Different trends require different trading strategies.

You shouldn't use a directional trading strategy in a range bound market. Similarly, you shouldn't use a range bound strategy for a directional trend.

Generally, in a range bound market, the goal is to buy weakness and sell into strength. In a directional trending market, the goal is to sell weakness and buy strength.

In an uptrend, you buy the pullbacks. In a downtrend, you sell the rallies.

4 - Support And Resistance

Stock prices are essentially determined by supply and demand. When there is more buying pressure than selling pressure, the stock price goes up. Or put another way, when there are more buyers than there are shares available at the current price, buyers must pay a higher price to get shares, which drives the price higher. The opposite is the case when the price of a stock drops. In this case, there are more sellers than buyers.

If the stock price goes high enough, it eventually reaches a point where buyers feel it has gotten too expensive, so they quit buying. This is referred to as *resistance*. The stock price resists going any higher. It's also referred to as hitting a *ceiling*.

Alternatively, the same is true when the price of a stock falls. At some point, it becomes sufficiently inexpensive that buyers will once again start buying. The stock is said to have *support* at the price where this occurs. It is also called a *floor*.

As shown on the preceding chart, the price bounces at the swing lows where support has been established, and pulls back when it encounters resistance at the swing highs. Of course, support and resistance levels are established and broken over time. This topic is covered in more detail later.

Confirming Support And Resistance

Support and resistance must be confirmed to be valid.

Notice on the chart that the stock was in an uptrend before pulling back and creating a swing point low. The price then had a reactive move to the upside. Afterwards, it fell and bounced at the swing low a second time. It successfully 'tested' or 'held' the swing low, which confirmed the support level.

For a period of time the price continued to bounce each time it fell back and hit the swing point low, further validating the support and establishing a solid floor. Unlike trendlines, support does not have to be validated three times. However, the greater number of times it is validated, the stronger the support becomes.

You may recall that I mentioned trends have persistence, meaning a trend is more likely to continue than reverse. The same is true of support. Support is more likely to hold than break. And, the stronger the support, the more likely it will hold.

Here is an example of support using a Candlestick chart (also, see "Candlestick Patterns" in the "Chart Patterns" chapter for more about candle variations).

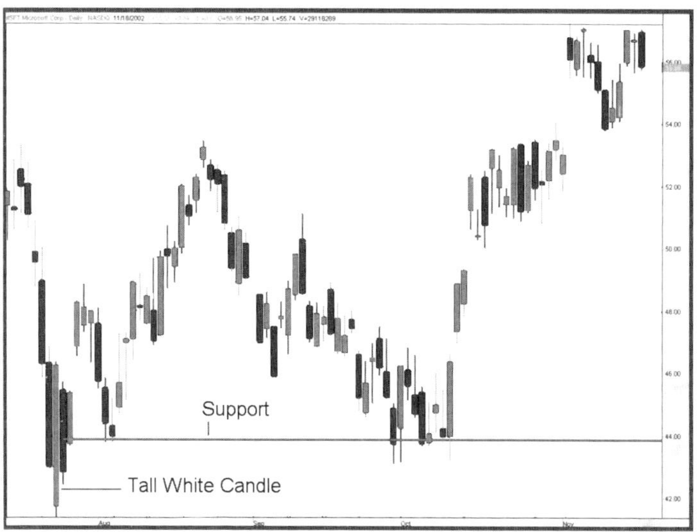

With Candlestick charts, a 'tall' white candle is an indication of support. Though the entire candle can be an area of support, the strongest support tends to occur in the top half of the candle (upper 50% range). For an example, see the preceding chart. Look for the support line that has been drawn at the midpoint of the tall white candle, which is located on the left side of the chart. Notice that the price repeatedly tests and holds the support. Tall candles are typically associated with an impulsive move, and they can also indicate that a trend reversal may be coming.

The same process that was described above for support is also true for resistance. Notice on the previous illustration that the price creates a swing high point. The price then falls back temporarily, bounces, and retests the swing high. The swing high holds a second time, which confirms the resistance. The swing high continues to hold with subsequent bounces, which further validates the resistance and establishes a solid ceiling.

With Candlestick charts, tall dark candles indicate areas of resistance. As with tall white candles, the entire tall dark candle can be an area of resistance, however, the strongest resistance tends to occur in the bottom 50% range of the candle.

See the following chart for an example.

Notice on the chart that the first test of the midpoint of the tall dark candle meets resistance that holds, the second swing high test doesn't get to the midpoint of the candle but it does make it into the bottom 50% range of the candle, which is also within the area of resistance.

Support And Resistance Trendlines

Trendlines can be used as support and resistance as long as they are defined by at least *three* swing points. A downtrend line is used for resistance, and an uptrend line is used for support.

Breakouts, Breakdowns, And Trend Reversals

At some point support and resistance will break. When support is broken, it's called a *breakout*. When resistance is broken, it's called a *breakdown* (although, breakout is often used for both).

Notice the downtrend line in the preceding illustration. The resistance held for five swing highs, then the price broke through the trendline, which resulted in a breakout. Refer to the next illustration to see what happened after the Breakout.

Break And Confirm

A trend reversal occurs when the last price swing that is counter to a trend is greater than the prior swing of the trend. However, when this happens, it doesn't mean that you should automatically assume a trend has reversed and jump in with both feet, as some traders tend to do.

A breakout alone doesn't guaranty a trend has reversed. Also, remember trend persistency - meaning a trend is more likely to continue than reverse. And even when a long pronounced trend does break, sideways basing action is likely to occur for a while afterwards. Then the trend may continue or it may reverse. Notice on the following chart that the breakout failed to continue.

Since there is no way to be sure whether a breakout will follow through, waiting for confirmation of the breakout is the best approach.

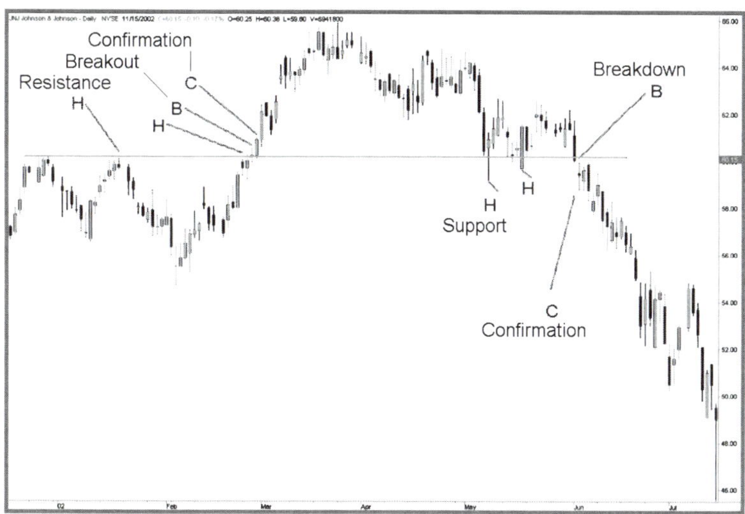

On the left side of the preceding chart, resistance has been established at the level indicated with an H. Then a break of the resistance occurs at point B. As in this case, breakouts often occur with a strong impulsive move. To confirm the breakout, wait for the next bar on the chart. If the next bar takes out the high of the breakout bar at point B, the breakout is confirmed. If you desire to trade the breakout, you could buy long after the confirmation at the C bar.

However, even after waiting for confirmation of a breakout, there is no guaranty the price won't subsequently pullback. Although the trade is correct, no trade is 100% foolproof and the action can still go against you. Therefore, you need to manage your trade and limit your potential risk exposure. You can do this by setting a stop-loss order slightly below the old resistance level. If the breakout fails to hold, you'll stop out of the trade with a minimal loss. If the price moves higher, adjust your stop-loss order accordingly and trail the price up to preserve profits.

The same process described above applies to confirming breakdowns as well, except the confirmation occurs when the low of next bar takes out the low of the breakdown bar, and you would go short to trade a breakdown. Your stop-loss order would be set slightly above the prior support level that was broken through, which now becomes resistance. See the second B and C on the right side of the prior chart for an example of a breakdown. The support at H is broken through to the downside.

Change Of Polarity

When a breakout or breakdown occurs and is confirmed, old resistance tends to become new support and old support tends to become new resistance. Steve Nison refers to this as the *change of polarity principle.*

Notice on the preceding chart that after resistance is broken, the price repeatedly bounced near the prior resistance level. The old resistance became the new support. Another example follows.

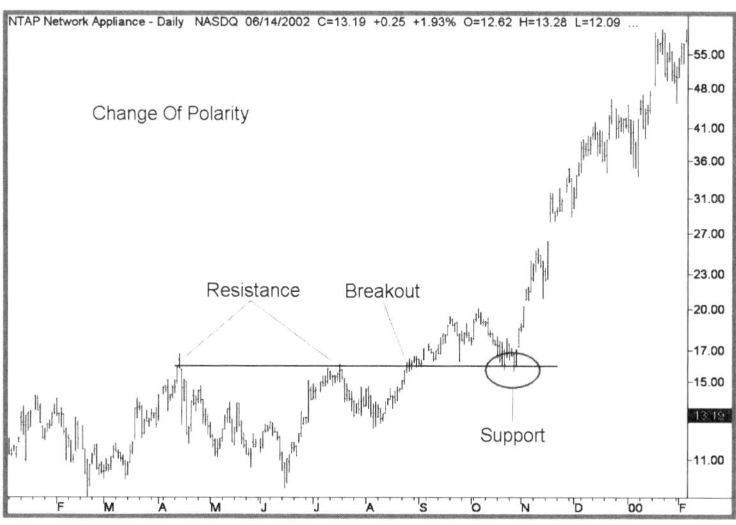

And here is an example that shows a breakdown of support.

Keeping old support and resistance lines on your charts can be very helpful and profitable, even several years later. Price has memory, so the starting points of previous bounces and declines often become inflection points for taking profits, or for timing the entries of trades.

5 - Volume

Volume is a popular leading technical indictor that shows the amount of interest in a particular stock, or in the market overall. It shows the quantity of shares that have been bought and / or sold over a period of time.

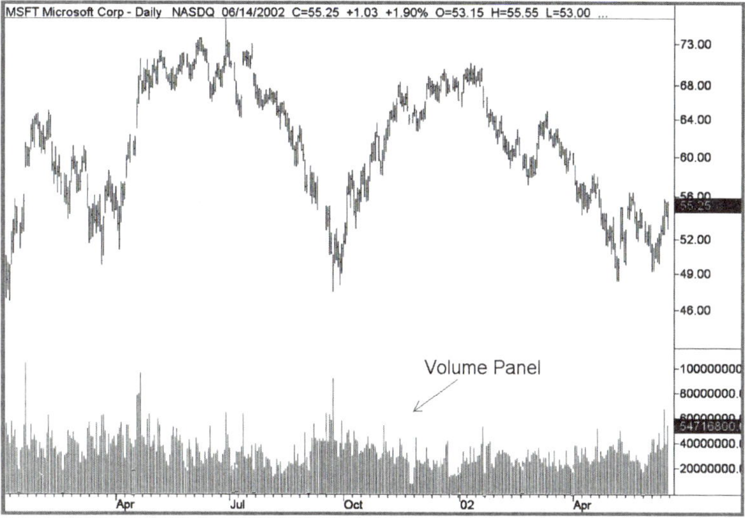

A volume panel is displayed at the bottom of the preceding chart.

Volume is an important indicator because it measures the amount of "crowd" participation in a stock. You should watch it closely, especially since the amount of crowd participation can have a major impact on price movement. You can think of volume as the *horsepower of price movement.*

Volume also shows the amount of institutional participation in a move. Contrary to what many believe, the daytraders, or "little guys", do not cause the large volume price moves. Instead, large institutional traders putting money to work or taking money out of the market cause the large moves.

Momentum And Impulse

Momentum is movement in a specific direction that continues to build upon itself, while *impulse* refers to an increase in a stock's momentum. Impulses can result from breakouts, a break of a directional trend, news or other events.

Momentum indicates the amount of relative strength or power behind a price movement. Both momentum and impulses are usually accompanied by a corresponding increase in volume.

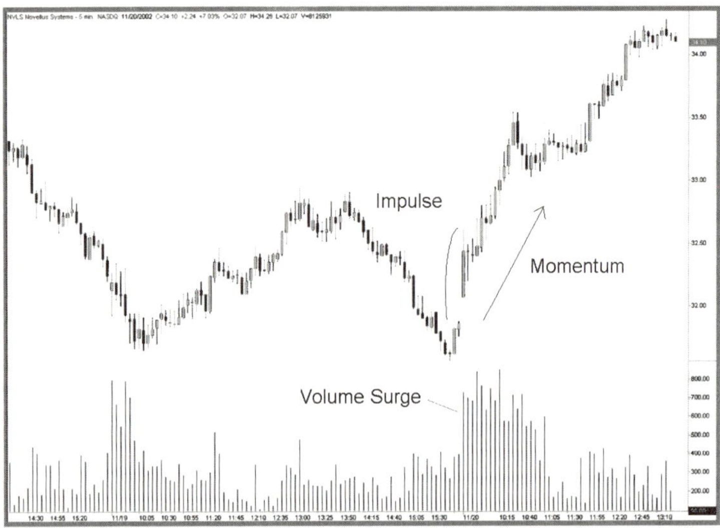

Momentum is a *leading* technical indicator, meaning it leads the market, which can give you an edge by providing an advance indication of a potential price move. Since momentum leads, new momentum highs are often followed by new price highs, and new momentum lows are often followed by new price lows.

In an uptrend, when momentum wanes, you may want to consider getting out of a long position, and/or consider whether to enter a short position. When momentum wanes in a downtrend, you may want to consider getting out of a short position, and/or consider whether to enter a long position. This doesn't mean that you should immediately close or enter a position, but you could tighten a stop-loss on an existing position, or watch for other patterns that might indicate a top, bottom, or price reversal. In other words, you shouldn't allow the indicator alone to determine the trade, but you can use it as additional confirmation.

Volume Spikes

Spikes in volume are important indicators to watch for. The following chart shows some examples.

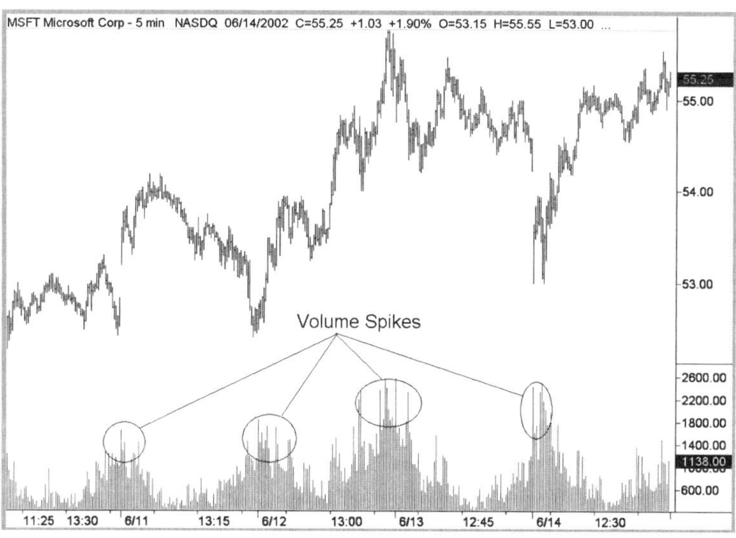

Volume spikes are indicators of short-term climaxes. They indicate the current leg of a trend may be about to end. If it's an uptrend, it could be a sign of a near term top. Since everyone is buying, the majority of buyers are likely in. If it's a downtrend, it could be a sign of a bottom. Since everyone is selling, the majority of sellers are probably out. When these climaxes occur, there is no one left to support the move.

Notice on the preceding chart how the volume spikes are associated with short-term tops and bottoms. The big climaxes are accompanied by increases in volume. After the climaxes, since the majority of people are now in or out of the stock, the volume drops off.

If the volume is associated with an impulsive move up, not only does the volume tend to fall afterwards, so does the price. Prices can fall from increased selling, or from decreased buying, as can be seen by the corresponding price and volume drops after the buying climaxes on the preceding chart. The opposite occurs with selling climaxes.

Volume is an important indicator for traders. The greater the volume is, the greater and stronger the move. Also, the greater the volume is, the greater the liquidity, another important consideration. Traders look for stocks with good momentum and liquidity so they can get in and out of trades easily and quickly. Strong momentum usually results in larger price swings as well, which makes it easier to profit from a trade.

See the areas indicated with an A on the following chart. There is a move up on low volume. Since there is not much volume or horsepower supporting the move, it is more suspect whether the move can be sustained. It doesn't mean you can't trade the uptrend, but you should trade more cautiously and watch long positions carefully, or not buy long at all if the stock has already made a large move on low volume. In fact, if you couldn't get in early on the move, it would be best to wait and watch for an opportunity to sell short on the downside leg when the uptrend breaks down.

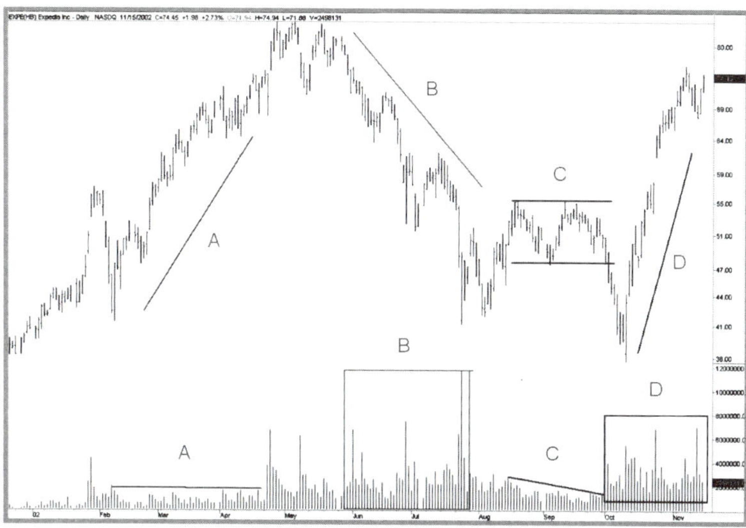

Referring to the chart once again, notice that a buying climax occurs at the top with a small, but noticeable volume spike. Then the stock eventually sells off on higher volume. See the areas marked with a B.

Later, the price goes into a range on low volume (area C), indicating interest in the stock has dried up. This is the type of setup you can watch for a trading opportunity. In the preceding example, two opportunities occur. One opportunity occurs when the range support level (end of C) is broken to the downside on high volume, and the other occurs when there is a breakout above the top of the range during the subsequent move to the upside. You could have sold short on the break to the downside. And, you could have entered a long position on the upside breakout (areas marked by D).

Finally, you can use volume to help gauge the strength of a breakout or breakdown. When either occurs with a corresponding surge in volume, the break is much stronger and more likely to continue, particularly when the surge in volume is 50% more than the 50-day volume moving average.

Since volume is such an important and commonly used indicator, you'll encounter additional information about its use throughout the book as applicable. Additionally, you can refer to the "Accumulation And Distribution" chapter, the "Volume MA" section of the "Moving Averages" chapter, and the "Volume Indicators" section for more information related to volume usage.

6 - Accumulation And Distribution

Accumulation is the buying of shares by people or institutions over a period of time to build up a position in a stock or other security, and distribution is the selling of shares over a period of time to reduce or liquidate a position.

When a large quantity of shares is involved, as is often the case with institutional transactions, shares are accumulated or distributed in smaller amounts over a period of time in an effort to avoid driving the market price up or down excessively.

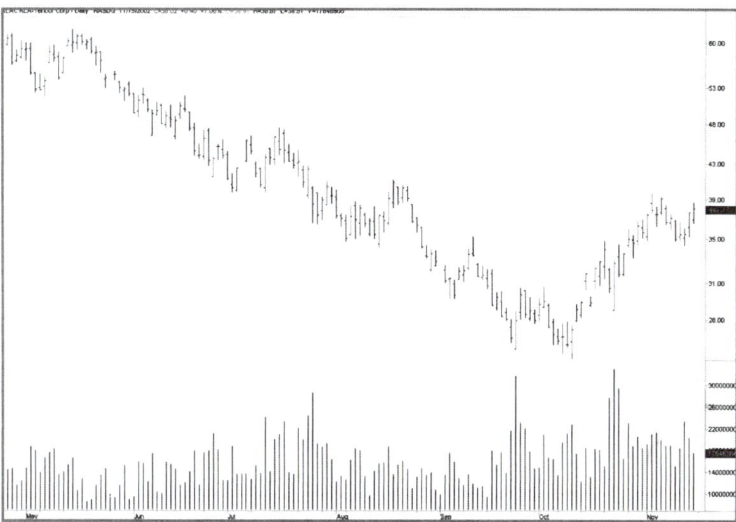

You can watch a stock's volume to determine whether it is being accumulated or distributed. An accumulation day occurs when the price

of a stock closes higher, and on higher volume, than it did on the prior day. Distribution occurs when the price of a stock closes lower, and on higher volume, than it did the prior day.

It's desirable to see accumulation days during an uptrend. Although a distribution day sprinkled here and there in an uptrend generally isn't cause for concern, too many distribution days during an uptrend should be considered a red flag. It indicates institutions and other sellers are using the higher prices to get out of their positions, so the move up may not last. It doesn't necessarily mean the uptrend won't continue, but it does merit more caution. You might want to consider reducing your position or maintaining a tighter stop-loss order.

Conversely, the opposite of the above is the case for downtrends. For the downtrend to continue, you want to see mostly distribution days. Too many accumulation days would indicate buying, so the downtrend could be coming to an end.

You can also use the On Balance Volume (OBV) indicator to help determine whether a stock is being accumulated over a period of time. The OBV indicator is covered later in the "Volume Indicators" section.

7 - Moving Averages

A *moving average* (or MA) is the average price of a stock over a specified period of time. Since moving averages smooth out price fluctuations, they are useful trend indicators. Traders also watch popular moving averages because of their potential to form key levels of support and resistance for a stock's price.

There are many types of calculations used to plot moving averages. Some that you may have heard about include: simple, exponential, triangular, weighted, and adaptive. I prefer to use only the first two types mentioned.

The Bull / Bear Barometer

The 200-day MA is the most widely watched moving average.

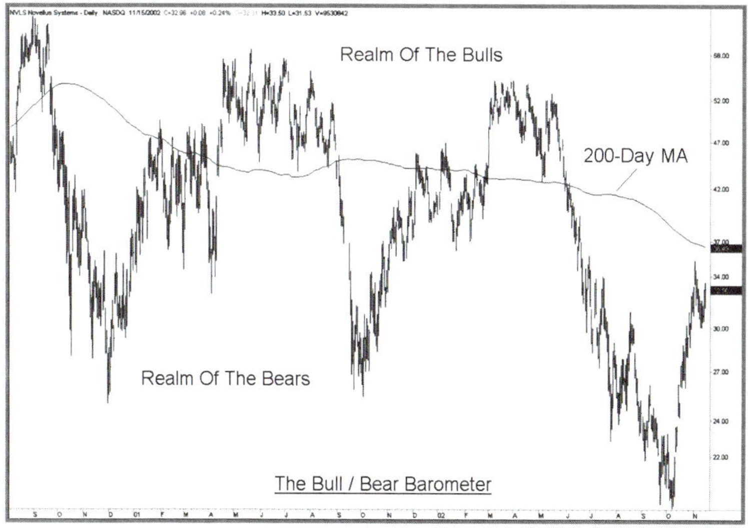

Institutional managers, hedge fund managers, traders, and the media (even those that preach the evils of technical analysis) all watch the 200-day MA. It is a benchmark moving average, which is why I refer to it as *The Bull / Bear Barometer*. If the price of a stock is above the 200-day MA, it's considered to be in a bull phase. Conversely, if the price is below the 200-day MA, it's considered a bear phase.

Key MAs

Institutions and traders watch certain key MAs closely for potential price pivots off of support and resistance, and for potential breakouts above or below the MAs. The key moving averages are:

- 10 day MA
- 20 day EMA
- 50 day MA
- 200 day MA

The 10-day MA is a short term two-week MA (5 days per week). The 20-day EMA is based upon a slightly longer timeframe of about one month. The 50-day MA is an intermediate term of about 2-1/2 months. And, as mentioned earlier, the 200-day MA is a key long term moving average.

An *exponential moving average* (EMA) tends to put more weight toward the end of a specified time period, and a *simple moving average* (SMA) is smoother throughout the time period. While prices are leading indictors, moving averages are lagging indicators. MA lines are plotted from historical market data, and current prices reflect what is actually happening at the present time in the market. A chart that shows the key moving averages follows.

Moving averages are useful trend indicators. For example, you can use a 50-day MA to see how a stock is trending for an intermediate time period, and a 10-day MA for a short-term trend.

MA Support And Resistance

MAs are frequently used as potential support and resistance levels.

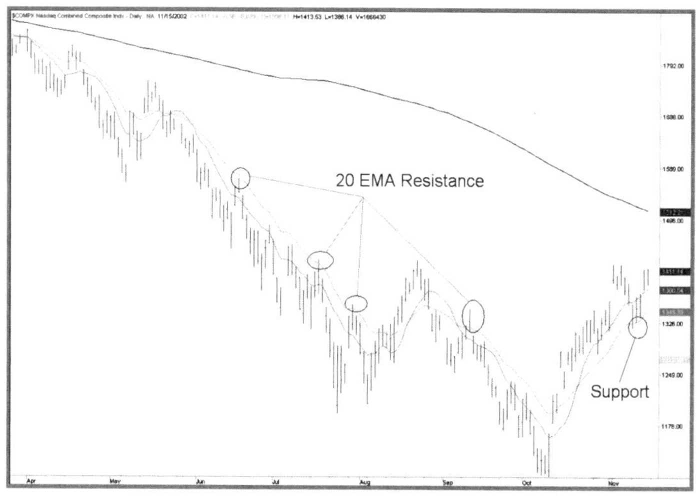

Notice on the preceding chart that the downtrend repeatedly met resistance at the 20-day exponential moving average. Often, when the price tested the 20-day EMA in the downtrend phase, it fell back. Eventually, the price broke above the 20-day EMA, and then subsequently bounced off of it. Similar to other support and resistance levels, the old resistance at the 20-day EMA became new support after the breakout occurred.

As with the 20-day EMA, you can watch all key moving averages for their potential to become an area of support or resistance.

Volume MA

You can use a moving average on the volume panel to help see the trend of the volume. With an MA line overlaid on the volume panel, a quick glance let's you see whether the volume is increasing, decreasing, or staying the same over a period of time.

Volume bars that spike above the 50-day moving average are said to be signs of institutional activity. These should grab your attention and peak your interest in the stock or market you are analyzing.

8 - Chart Patterns

Charts are used to analyze various types of pattern formations in market data. Once you learn how to recognize the patterns, you can use them to help time the entries and exits for your trades.

The price movements that apply to trading patterns are breakouts, retracements, and tests. Using charts, you can analyze the patterns and price movements then plan appropriate trading strategies.

This chapter introduces you to a variety of chart patterns and offers suggestions for trading them.

Double Tops And Bottoms

The following illustration shows a *Double Top* pattern.

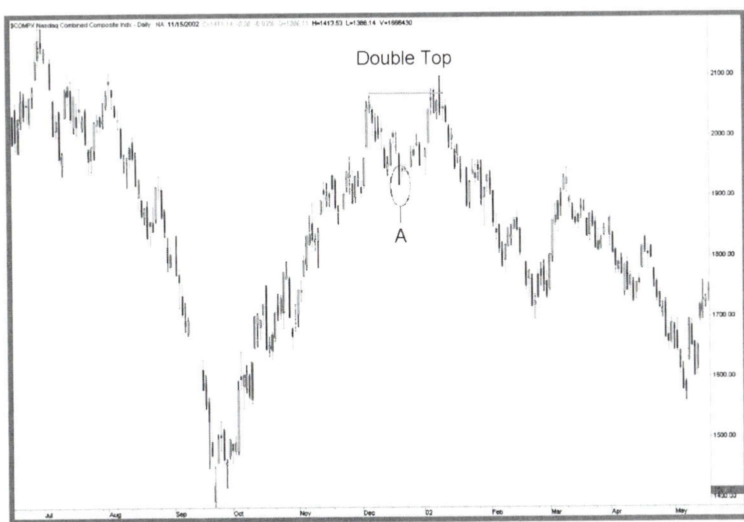

Referring to the preceding chart, notice that during the uptrend leg of the Double Top, higher highs and higher lows are made until a swing high is created at the left side of the Double Top. This is followed by a pullback. However, the pullback results in a swing low that is higher than the prior swing low (see point A on the chart). Afterwards, there's another push to the upside that retests the prior high of the Double Top. If the resistance of the prior high holds, the potential for a Double Top remains intact (note that a small amount of variation is okay). Finally, another pullback breaks through the prior low at the valley of the Double Top (point A). Once the valley low is broken through, a Double Top is confirmed.

At this point, you could trade the pattern by selling short right after the Double Top is confirmed (i.e., after the breakdown of the valley low).

The above approach is the true entry for the trade; however, you could 'cheat' an entry right after the second swing high of the Double Top is tested. You would then place a stop-loss slightly above the Double Top resistance just in case a true Double Top isn't confirmed and the price moves higher rather than lower.

If you flip a Double Top upside down, you will have a *Double Bottom*. Double Bottoms are confirmed and traded the same way as previously described for Double Tops, except the process is reversed.

Referring to the following example, you would enter the trade by going long when the final leg of the Double Bottom breaks out above the swing high at point A on the chart.

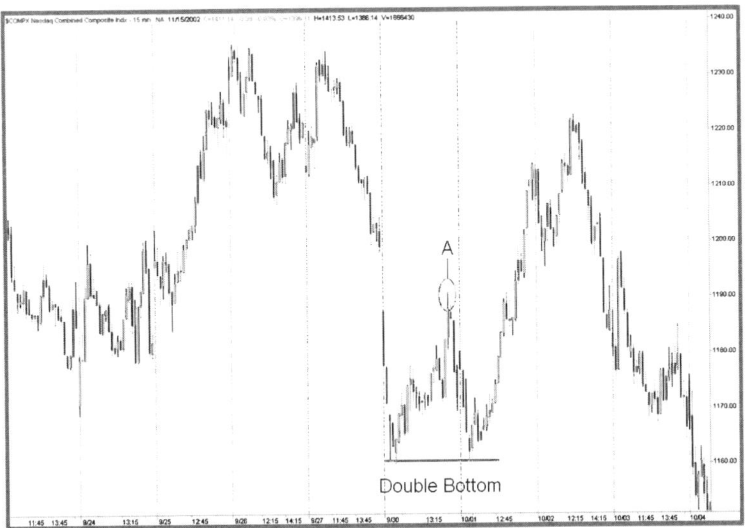

Also, notice on the chart that a Double Top precedes the Double Bottom. Even though the second leg of the Double Top didn't quite make it all the way up to the swing high of the first leg, you could still trade the move by selling short once the Double Top valley low is broken to the downside. You wouldn't be able to 'cheat' the entry in this case, since the second leg of the Double Top didn't confirm the resistance that was created by the first leg.

Head & Shoulders

A *Head & Shoulders* bears some resemblance to a Double Top, except it has a third swing high point in the center rather than a valley.

Refer to the following example. Notice that the Head & Shoulders consists of a swing high in the center (the Head) that is surrounded by two lower swing highs (the Shoulders).

The Shoulders do not need to be precisely the same height, and the swing low points at the bottom of the Head & Shoulders (or neckline) need not be perfect either, though they should be reasonably close. The neckline at the base of the Head & Shoulders forms the support level. A break of the neckline confirms an entry for a short trade. Therefore, a Head & Shoulders is a bearish indicator.

Sometimes after the break of the neckline, you'll get a snapback bounce back up to the neckline, which creates a second opportunity to enter the trade. The neckline becomes the resistance for the snapback bounce. Refer to the previous chart for an example.

Note, however, that sometimes a snapback may exceed the neckline, which is okay as long as the snapback doesn't take out the nearest Shoulder's swing high. If it does take out the swing high of the Shoulder, then the Head & Shoulders is no longer valid.

A possible third 'cheat' entry for a Head & Shoulders trade is at the point where the pullback occurs after the second shoulder makes its swing high point. You could enter a short position at that time.

A Head & Shoulders Measured Move

You can measure the potential downside move that occurs after the break of a Head & Shoulders neckline.

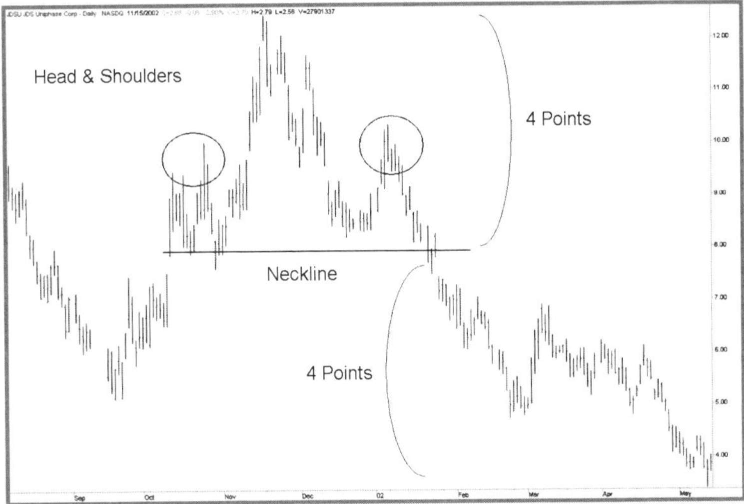

Referring to the preceding illustration, measure the distance (or price difference) between the neckline and the swing high of the head. The break of the neckline to the downside has the potential to move the same distance. So, if the distance between the neckline and swing high of the head was 4 points, you could set a profit target of 4 points for your trade. Once you hit your target, though, you should take profits, or take part of your profits and set a tighter stop-loss order on the rest of your position.

Inverted Head & Shoulders

An *Inverted Head & Shoulders* is essentially an upside down Head & Shoulders.

Since a Head & Shoulders is a bearish indicator, an Inverted Head & Shoulders is bullish.

To confirm and trade an Inverted Head & Shoulders, simply reverse all of the procedures previously described for the Head & Shoulders pattern.

When the last leg of the Inverted Head & Shoulders breaks out above the inverted neckline, you can enter a long position. The other conditions described previously apply as well. That is, you could get a snapback after a breakout; you could do a measured move; and you could consider a 'cheat' entry after the second Shoulder's swing point low is confirmed.

Cup & Handle

The *Cup & Handle* pattern was invented and popularized by William O'Neil in his book *"How To Make Money In Stocks"*. It has gained wide acceptance as a very reliable chart pattern.

Textbook Cup & Handles don't occur very often so with some slight modifications, it's more likely you'll find one that can be traded successfully.

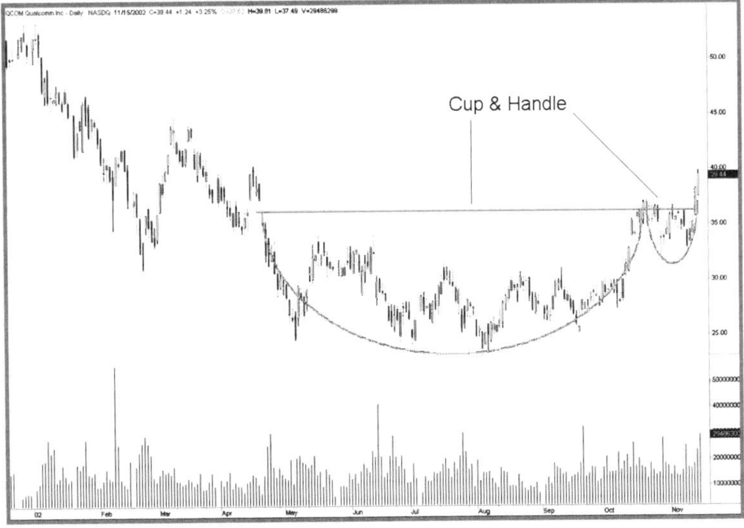

The preceding chart shows a Cup & Handle. To find a Cup & Handle, you look for range action with a rounded bottom. Each side of the Cup should have reasonably close swing point highs. These form the resistance level for the top of the Cup. Next, a smaller rounded-bottom range forms the Handle of the Cup, as seen in the previous example. The Handle shouldn't retrace downward by more than 50% of the depth of the Cup.

When the Handle breaks through resistance, you can buy the breakout. This is such a strong play that you can even do it without confirmation, but if you do, I suggest trading only one-half your normal lot size to minimize risk. Alternatively, you can wait for the first pullback after the breakout as confirmation. You'll often get a snapback after the breakout. If support holds after the first pullback (or holds reasonably close), the breakout is confirmed and you can enter your trade. Since old resistance becomes new support, the support level is the old resistance, or the top of the Cup.

There is such a thing as an inverted Cup & Handle, however, they are harder to spot and they tend not to be as reliable so I generally don't trade them.

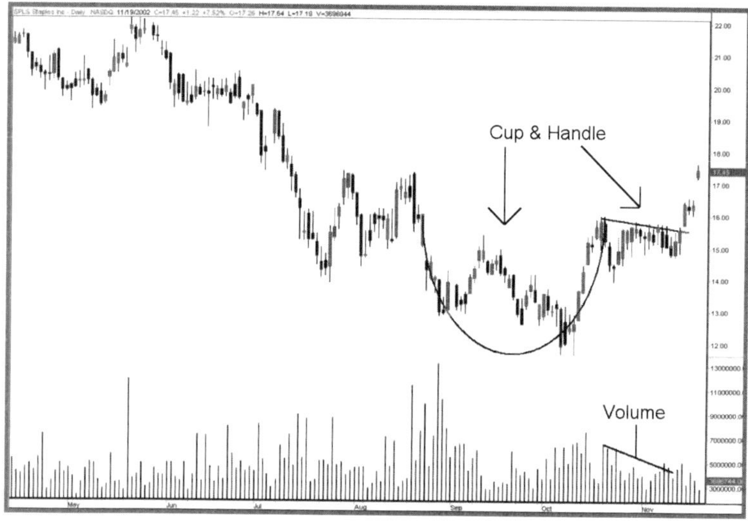

Volume can also be used as an indicator to further confirm a Cup & Handle trade. What you look for is a Handle that forms on decreasing volume, as shown on the preceding chart. You may recall that a range breakout often occurs after interest in a stock has dried up. So, if you spot this and pay attention, you might enter the trade ahead of everyone else then you can ride the initial impulse surge that occurs when the buyers come back in. It's best to be cautious, however, and wait for confirmation then use a stop-loss order, but it is another indicator you can use to help time your entry.

Triangle

A *Triangle* is generally just a basing pattern rather than a trending one. When a Triangle begins to form, it indicates a stock is coming to an equilibrium point. Since a Triangle is a consolidation pattern, there is no directional bias. The bias occurs when the stock moves out of the triangle.

When you see a triangle forming, it indicates a stock is about to make a move that could provide a good trading opportunity. It is time to pay attention!

Symmetrical Triangle

The following chart shows a Symmetrical Triangle.

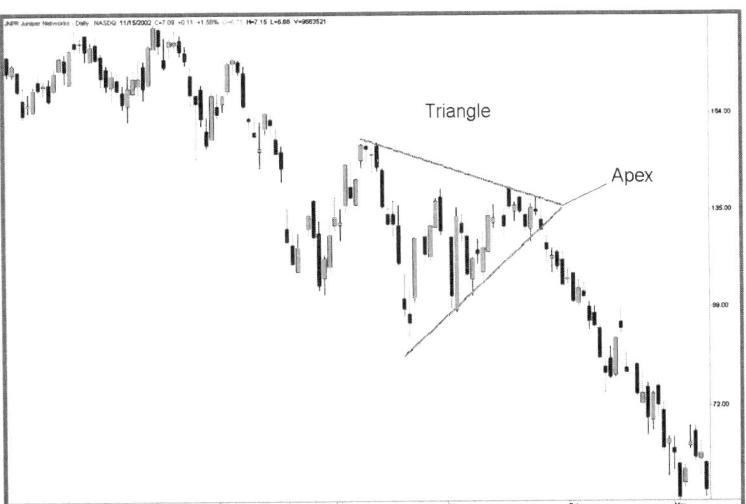

A Symmetrical Triangle has a rising trendline and a declining trendline. You may recall that a trendline needs to touch three points to be valid. On a Triangle, only one of the trendlines needs to touch three or more points, either the uptrend line or the downtrend line. The apex of the Triangle is the point where the two trendlines meet. Notice the swing lengths between the swing highs and swing lows get shorter nearer the apex.

Symmetrical Triangles tend to breakout or breakdown about 2/3 of the way into the Triangle. When this occurs, the move is more likely to be a large dynamic move.

In cases where the move simply dribbles out the end of the apex, it still may evolve into a trending move; however, it may be preceded by a false move. For that reason, it's best to wait for a retest of the apex, and a resumption of the trend before entering a trade. When the move slowly dribbles out of the apex there tends to be no momentum behind the move, and a reversal often occurs when there is no momentum. An example of an apex exit is shown under the *"Ascending Triangle"* section, which comes next.

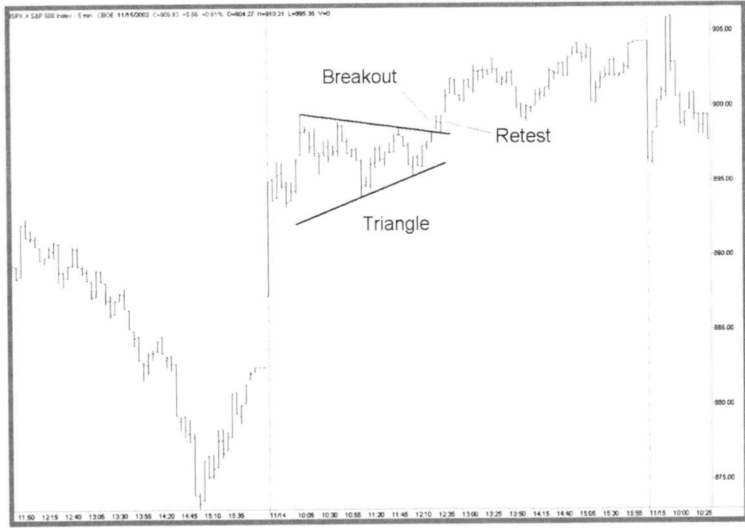

A breakout of a Triangle can be to the upside or the downside. However, a breakout to the downside is technically called a breakdown. Notice on the preceding chart, there is a breakout to the upside then the next bar immediate retests the trendline.

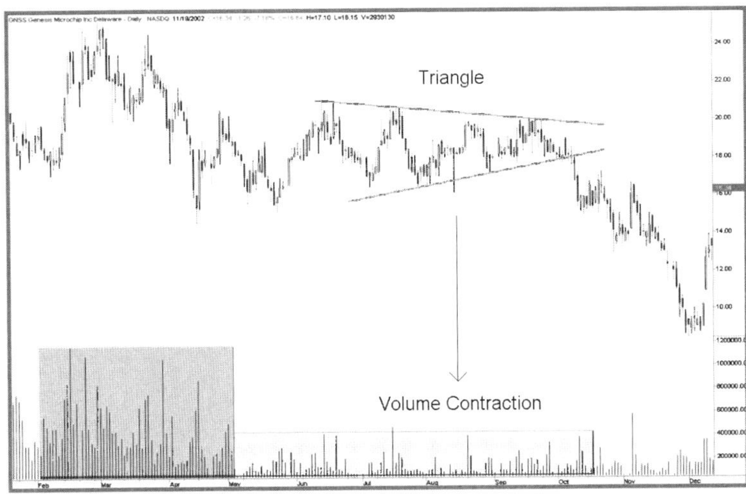

When a Triangle forms, volume usually contracts because the price action tends to be range bound, which results in a loss of interest in the stock. See the volume panel on the preceding chart. Notice how the volume contracted during the formation of the Triangle.

Ascending Triangle

An *Ascending Triangle* has a flat trendline on the top and a rising trendline on the bottom.

Notice how the price movement dribbles out of the apex, then pulls back slightly before moving higher. As mentioned previously, in cases where the move simply dribbles out of the apex, it is more likely to evolve into a trending move; however, it may be preceded by a false move. For that reason, it's best to wait for a retest of the apex, and a resumption of the trend before entering a trade. When the move slowly dribbles out of the apex there tends to be no momentum behind the move, and a reversal often occurs when there is no momentum.

Descending Triangle

The top trendline for a *Descending Triangle* slopes down, while the bottom trendline is flat.

Notice that a breakdown occurs about two-thirds of the way into the Triangle, and then there is a brief snapback before the fall continues.

Pennant

A *Pennant* is a small triangular pattern with very few distinct swings within it. For that reason, a Pennant does not need to touch three points on either of its trendlines.

The following chart shows an example of a Pennant.

While a Triangle is a consolidation pattern, a Pennant is a continuation pattern. In order to have a continuation pattern, it must be preceded by an impulsive move. Notice the impulsive move just ahead of the Pennant on the preceding chart. Frequently, Pennants will breakout in the direction of the trend. If an impulse was to the upside, the breakout of the Pennant will likely be to the upside as well.

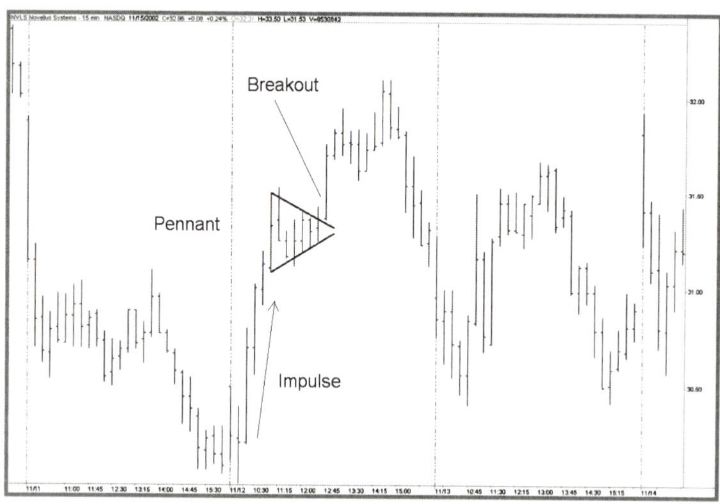

The preceding illustration shows an intraday Pennant, which can also be traded very successfully. Notice the required impulsive move up that precedes the Pennant. The Pennant forms, then there is a strong, impulsive breakout to the upside. Another example follows.

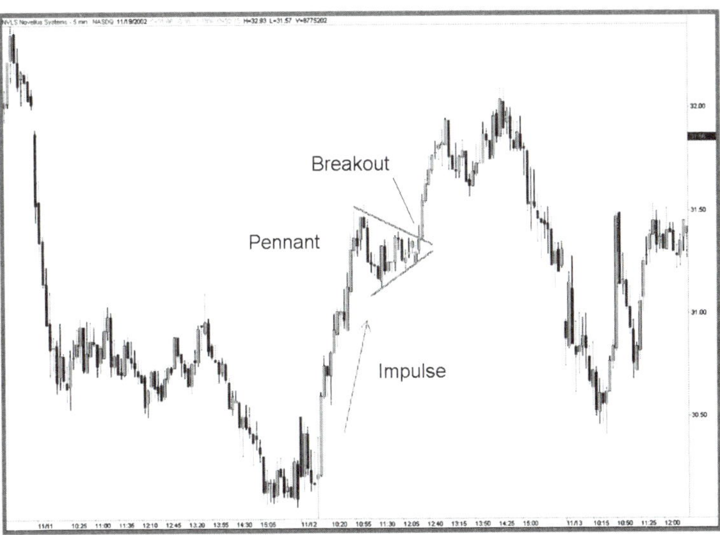

You do not need to confirm a Pennant breakout. You could enter a trade at the point where the Pennant breaks out above the upper trendline, and then set a stop-loss order beneath the lower trendline (directly beneath the point where the breakout occurred).

If the Pennant fails, meaning the move falls below the lower trendline, you should stop out of the trade because the Pennant is no longer valid.

As shown on the next chart, Pennants often occur after a dynamic range breakout. Notice the nice basing action, then a Pennant forms after a strong impulsive breakout.

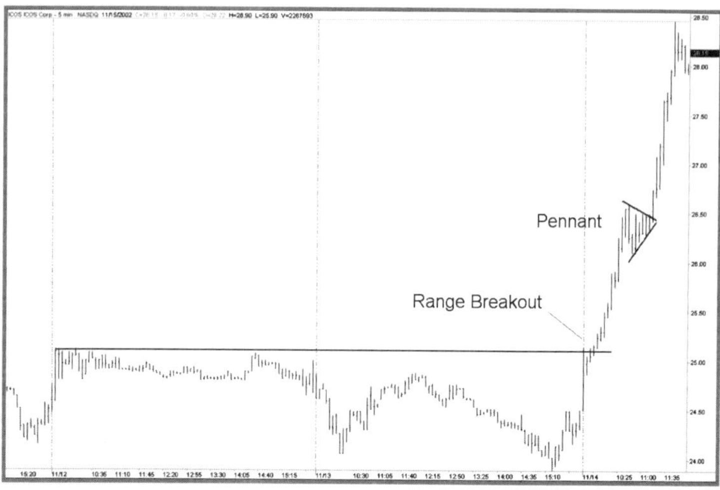

If you didn't get in on the initial range breakout, you could enter a long position for a nice continuation move higher after the Pennant breaks out. As with a Triangle, the chart that follows shows how volume tends to dry up as a Pennant is formed; since a Pennant is also range consolidation.

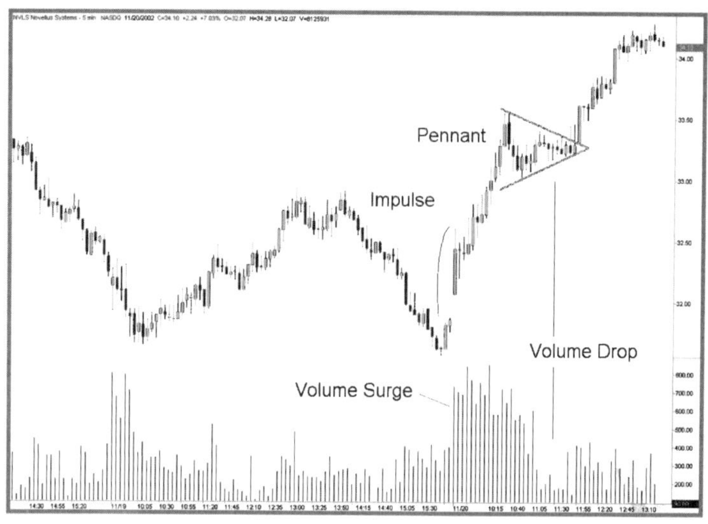

Also notice on the preceding chart that the swing high point ahead of the Pennant is larger than the previous swing high, which further validates entering a long position after a breakout of the Pennant.

The following chart shows an intraday pennant. Notice the same characteristics as before. There is a strong impulsive move prior to the forming of the Pennant. Then, there is a strong continuation breakout of the Pennant.

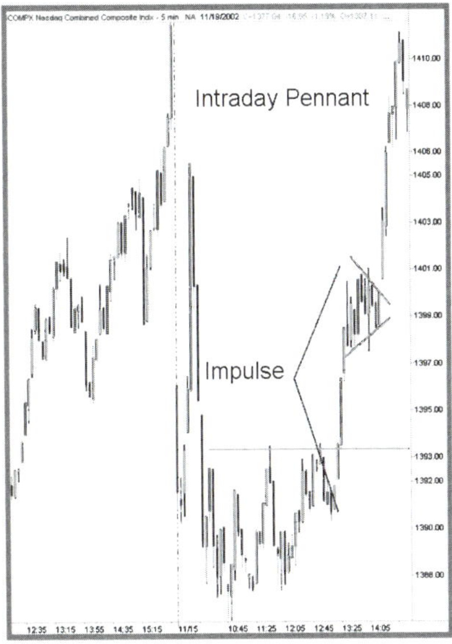

These Pennants provide great intraday trading opportunities. With such a strong impulsive move, you could go long ahead of the apex of the Pennant, with a stop-loss order placed beneath the Pennant.

Flags

While Pennant patterns provide great trading opportunities, *Flags* provide even better opportunities. In fact, it is possible to make a living by trading only Flags. In my opinion, they are the most consistently profitable pattern to trade, and I urge you to learn all you can about Flags then watch for the opportunities they provide.

Like Pennants, volume tends to dry up as Flags are formed, and Flags must be preceded by an impulsive move. Remember, the length of the impulsive swing must be greater than the length of the swing that precedes it.

A Flag generally moves counter to the direction of the impulsive move, but not always. Flags that move sideways to, or in the same direction as, an impulsive move often result in even stronger breakouts.

If an impulse does not precede a flag, it could just be a general continuation pattern. Regardless, it is not a true Flag. This may just seem like semantics, but it is more than that. I feel that a true Flag is one of the most powerful patterns that exist in technical analysis; therefore, do not settle for anything less than the correct pattern.

For a Flag to be valid it should contain at least three bars.

Bull Flag

A *Bull Flag* often forms after an impulsive upside breakout of resistance.

Notice on the following chart that an impulsive move to the upside breaks through the resistance, and the length of the swing up is greater than the prior swing down. The first pullback forms a Bull Flag consisting of three bars. At least three are required but more is okay.

You can enter a trade long when a breakout of the Bull Flag's highest trendline occurs, with a stop-loss order set at the bottom of the Bull Flag.

Bear Flag

A *Bear Flag* forms with the same setup as a Bull Flag, except the initial impulsive move is to the downside.

On the preceding chart, an impulsive sell off occurs after the swing high is made, breaking through support. The length of the swing down is greater than the prior swing up (see A and B). A Bear Flag then forms, moving counter to the impulse. You can enter a short trade when a breakdown of the Bear Flag's lower trendline occurs, and set a stop-loss order at the top of the Bear Flag.

After the Bear Flag breaks down, notice that there is another small pullback, which is actually another Bear Flag. It may be small, but it is still a 3-bar Bear Flag that follows an impulsive move. Note that it is okay if a Bear Flag only has one trendline rather than two.

Candlestick Patterns

An explanation and example of candlestick charts is provided in the "Price Charts" chapter under "Japanese Candlestick Charts". This subsection describes individual candle appearances and what they mean.

As previously mentioned, the appearance of a candle varies in many subtle but very important ways. Candles come in a variety of colors, shapes and sizes, and these differences communicate important information.

Here is the general makeup of a candle.

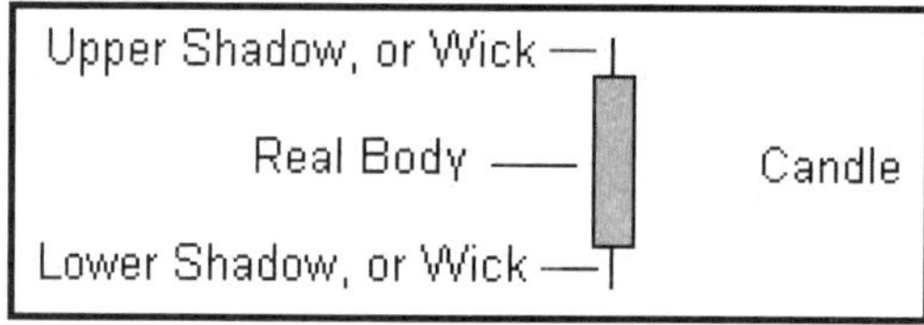

The thick part of a candle is called the real body. The top and bottom of the real body reflect the opening and closing prices for the interval's time period, and the shadows represent the highs and lows. These are all covered in more detail next.

When reading the following, keep in mind that candle colors can vary according to the charting software you use. Some charting software uses green for white candles. However, they could also be another custom color. The same is true of dark candles. They are often red but could be other colors.

Bullish White Candle

A white, or green, candle indicates the bulls dominated the price action. Here is an example of a white candle.

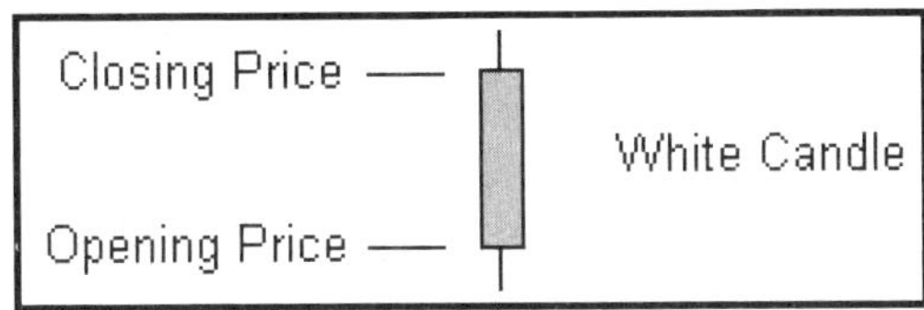

Since the opening price of a white candle is at the bottom of the real body and the closing price is at the top, it means there was likely excess buying pressure that pushed the price higher during the candle's time period.

Bearish Dark Candle

A dark, or red, candle indicates the bears dominated the price action.

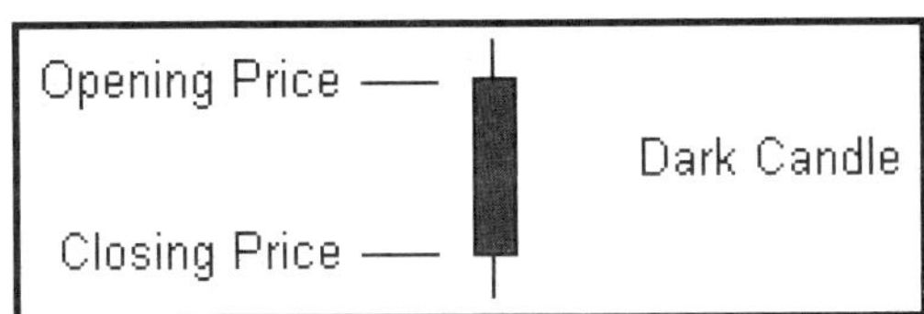

Since the opening price of a red candle is at the top of the real body and the closing price is at the bottom, it means there was likely excess selling pressure that caused the price to fall during the candle's time period.

Spinning Top

Spinning Tops are neither bullish nor bearish. Instead, the bulls and bears are in a tug of war. Notice the length of the shadows relative to the size of the real body.

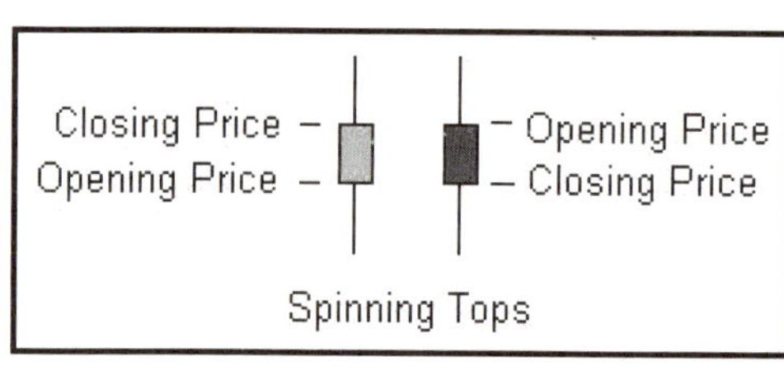

You'll often see Spinning Tops when a stock is stuck in a range and moving sideways. During an uptrend, a Spinning Top could be a sign the trend is losing momentum, so you should at least consider it a red flag and trade accordingly by adjusting your risk management parameters (e.g., tightening trailing stop-loss orders, reducing lot sizes, etc.).

Doji

A Doji consists mostly of shadows above and below the real body. The real body appears thin and flat, or short. It means the price opened and closed within a tight range, which once again indicates the bulls and bears are in a tug of war. However, if the stock has been in a directional trend, either up or down, a Doji could indicate a potential change of direction is on the way.

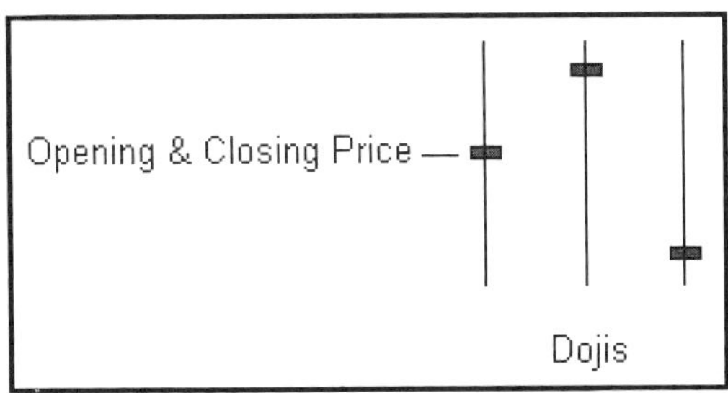

Dojis are very powerful indicators. When you see one, you should at least consider it a red flag. Some traders will even enter a trade or tighten stops based solely on seeing a Doji, particularly if the stock has been in a directional trend up to that point. There are different types of Dojis. For example, the shadow could be longer at the top or bottom, or it could be equal lengths above and below the real body. Or put another way, the real body may appear at the top, bottom, or in the center, which provides some additional indication as to the overall direction of the move when compared to adjacent candles (see "Shadow Lengths" below for more).

Shadow Lengths

Long upper shadows are bearish indicators, while long lower shadows are bullish. These are additional powerful indicators you can use to help determine when to enter or exit trades.

For example, if you are in a long position and see a very long upper shadow, even if the candle is white, it means the bears are still present. So, you should pay close attention and may even want to consider exiting your trade or tightening your stop-loss order. Alternatively, if you are looking to go short, it could be a good time to get ready to enter your trade.

In the case of a long lower shadow, if you are currently in a long position and are trying to decide whether to get out, you might want to consider waiting a little longer, since the Bulls are still present.

High Wave Candles

Both resembling a Spinning Top and similar to a Doji, the shadows are somewhat longer than a Spinning Top while the real body is slightly shorter; however, the real body is not as flat as a Doji.

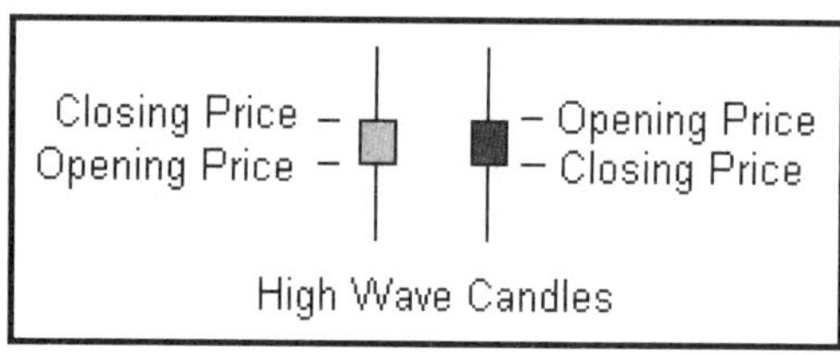

High Wave Candles indicate the market is in a standoff between the bulls and bears. It can indicate a lack of direction in the market. While it doesn't necessarily mean you should enter or exit a trade, you might want to pay a little closer attention, since a change of direction could be on the way.

Hammer

A Hammer has a very small stub as the upper shadow, and a long lower shadow. It has a short real body that is positioned at the top of the candle.

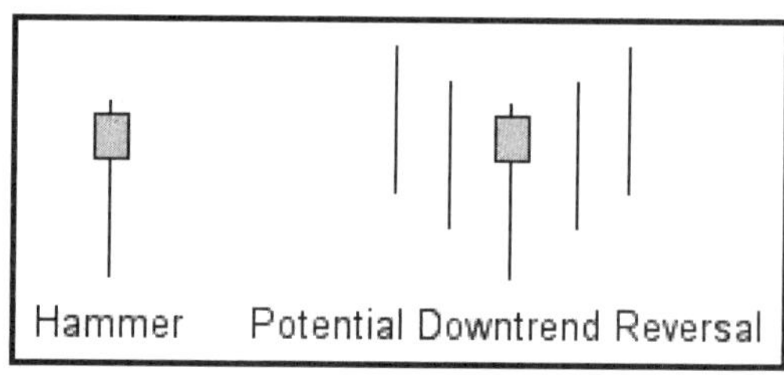

A Hammer is another powerful indicator of strong support, and often indicates the end of a significant downtrend. Confirmation occurs when the price breaks above the top of the Hammer.

While you don't necessarily want to jump in and trade a Hammer when in a sideways range, in a downtrend it is a great low risk, high percentage trade, especially when it occurs at a support level. You can enter a long position with defined risk by buying a break of the high of the hammer and putting a stop-loss order just below the bottom of the candle.

Hanging Man

A Hanging Man looks like a Hammer, except it occurs in a strong uptrend, which often indicates a reversal of the trend.

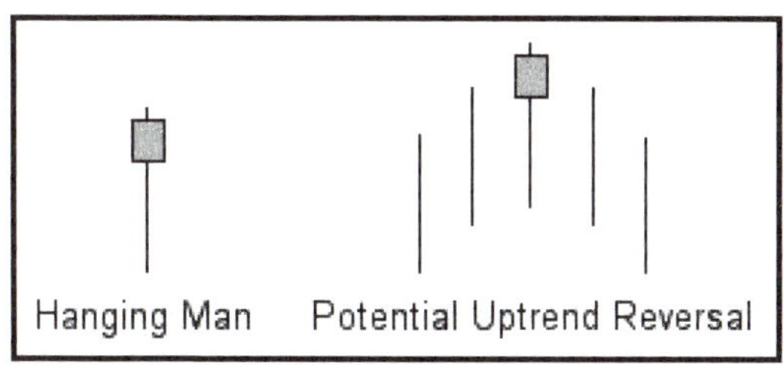

In this case, you could consider entering a short position on a break of the low of the Hanging Man with a stop-loss order just above the high of the candle to limit your risk. You should only do this in an uptrend, and not during a sideways range.

Also, keep in mind that since the long shadow of a Hanging Man is bullish, it's best to use it in conjunction with other indicators.

To be honest, I am not a big fan of the Hanging Man pattern but I still included it in the book for your personal consideration and to more fully differentiate the various types of candles.

Shooting Star

A Shooting Star looks like an upside down Hammer, or Inverted Hammer. It has a long upper shadow with a short stubby shadow underneath. This is a powerful bearish indicator, and is one of my favorite candlestick patterns to trade.

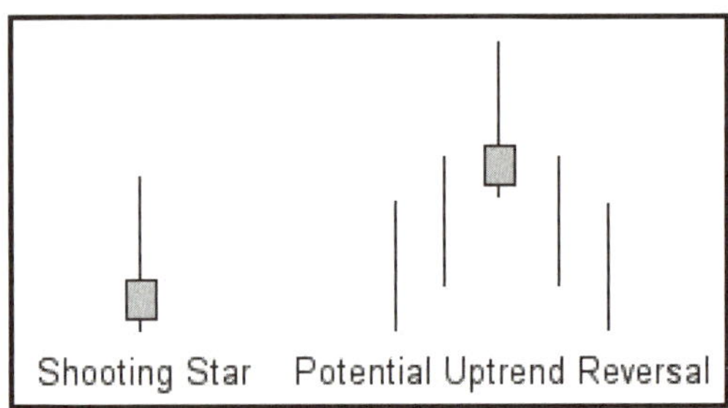

Since a Shooting Star is a very reliable indicator of an uptrend reversal, I prefer a Shooting Star over a Hanging Man. Upon seeing a Shooting Star during an uptrend, you could enter a short trade with limited risk by selling short on a break of the low of the Shooting Star and setting a stop-loss order slightly above the top of the candle.

Dark Cloud Cover

A Dark Cloud Cover is a two-candle bearish reversal pattern that may signal the end of an uptrend (see the next illustration).

The first candle is a strong white candle that is followed by a second dark candle. The dark candle opens above the white candle and closes below its midpoint, engulfing a portion of the white candle's body.

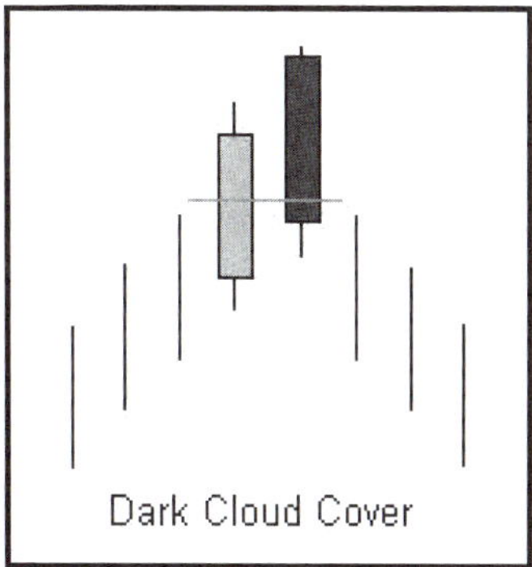

If the dark candle doesn't close below the midpoint of the white candle, the Dark Cloud Cover pattern is considered invalid. Generally, the lower the dark candle closes below the midpoint of the white candle, the more bearish the signal.

The following chart shows an example of a Dark Cloud Cover reversal.

An analysis of the pattern on the chart shows the following. The session starts with a gap up above the previous day's highs, but it closes below the previous day's close. This traps anxious breakout buyers who bought without confirmation. When the breakout buyers realize they are wrong, it helps fuel the reversal.

The Piercing Pattern

The Piercing Pattern is the opposite of a Dark Cloud Cover. It is a two-candle bullish reversal pattern that may signal the end of a downtrend.

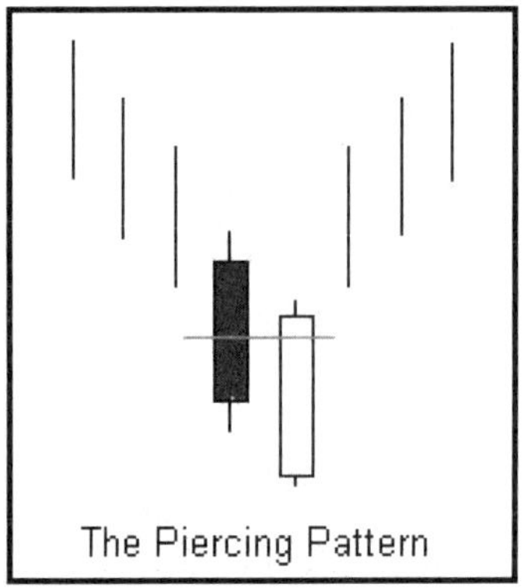
The Piercing Pattern

The first candle is a strong dark candle, which is followed by a second candle that is white. The white candle opens below the bottom of the dark candle, and must close above the dark candle's midpoint. Therefore, the white candle engulfs a portion of the dark candle's body.

The Piercing Pattern indicates buying is taking place at the lower levels of the pattern. The higher the white candle closes above the midpoint of the dark candle, the more bullish the signal.

The following chart shows a two-candle Piercing Pattern reversal.

An analysis of the pattern on the chart shows the following. The session starts with a gap down below the previous day's lows, but it closes above the previous day's close. This traps anxious breakdown sellers who sold without waiting for confirmation. Shame on them, but good for us! When the breakdown sellers realize that they are wrong and decide to buy to cover, it helps fuel the reversal, and often ignites a short-squeeze induced move as well.

Single-Candlestick Support

Candles can also indicate areas of support, as in the case of a tall white candle. Though the entire candle can be an area of support, the strongest support tends to occur at the top half of the candle (upper 50% range). For an example, on the following chart, refer to the support line that has been drawn at the midpoint of the tall white candle that's located on the left side of the chart. Notice that price repeatedly tests the support and it holds.

Tall candles are typically associated with an impulsive move, and they can indicate that a trend reversal may be coming

Single-Candlestick Resistance

In addition to indicating areas of support, candles can also indicate areas of resistance. See the tall dark candle on the following chart.

As with tall white candles, the whole candle can be an area of resistance, however, the strongest resistance occurs in the bottom 50% range of the tall dark candle. On the preceding chart, notice the first test of the midpoint of the tall dark candle encounters resistance that holds, and while the second swing high test doesn't get to the midpoint of the candle, it does make it into the bottom 50% range of the candle, which is also within the area of resistance.

Two-Candlestick Bullish Engulfing Pattern

The following chart shows a two-candle Bullish Engulfing Pattern.

On the chart, there is a dark candle followed by a taller white candle that both opens lower than the preceding dark candle, and closes higher. It *engulfs* or swallows up the dark candle. This is a very bullish indicator. As mentioned previously, the top half of a tall white candle also frequently establishes an area of support.

Upon confirmation of support, you could enter a long position with a stop-loss order slightly below the 50% support level to limit your risk exposure.

Two-Candlestick Bearish Engulfing Pattern

You can also have a Bearish Engulfing Pattern.

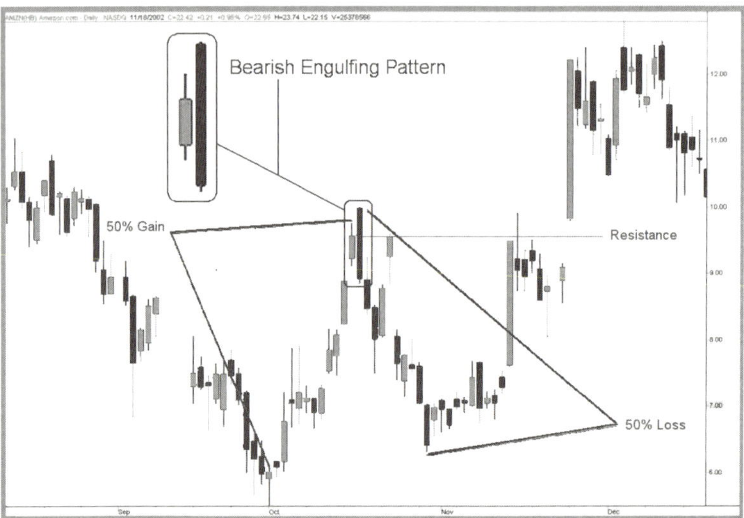

Near the center of the chart, you'll see a white candle that is engulfed by a taller dark candle. This is a bearish indicator. The price dropped by 50% after the tall dark candle appeared. While the entire dark candle is an area of resistance, the bottom 50% of the tall dark candle is the area of strongest resistance.

Upon confirmation of the resistance you could enter a short position. However, since the dark candle is not a particularly tall candle this time, it's best to use the top of the candle for a stop-loss order rather than putting it slightly above the midpoint. Also, note that a short position is only entered into in cases where the downtrend remains intact, that is, the swing to the upside is not greater than the prior swing to the downside. If it were, this would still be a bearish indicator, but rather than going short, you would use it as a warning sign to exit long positions.

About Candlesticks

There are many other types of Japanese Candlestick patterns, including three-candle patterns. However, the preceding group is a great place to start, and in my opinion, they are the most important patterns to learn.

If you would like to explore candlestick patterns further, there are plenty of good books dedicated entirely to Japanese Candlestick charting. Please remember, though, you can learn all of the fancy names and look for patterns all day, but a pattern is only as powerful as where it appears on a chart. For example, a Piercing Pattern at the top of an uptrend has no forecasting power, and a Doji in the middle of a trend doesn't signal a reversal. When you see a candlestick pattern, ask yourself the following question: "What trend are we in?". This will keep you in the right state of mind while doing your analysis.

9 - Gaps

A *gap* occurs when a stock's price opens outside of its range from the previous day. A gap up occurs when a stock's price opens above its high from the previous day. A gap down occurs when a stock's price opens below its low from the previous day.

A gap is a form of impulse, and the reaction of the stock after a gap in either direction should be studied carefully for clues of continuation or reversal.

It is a common misconception that all gaps get filled. This is not always true. Often, a gap can be the start of a dynamic move, and the price never returns to fill the gap. For example, if you check the tops of many of the "high-flyers" from the late 1990s, you will see many stocks have price gaps that will never be filled.

Laps

Although the term gap is most often used; there are forms of gaps that technically should be called laps. A lap occurs when a stock's price opens within its previous day's range (high and low), but above or below its previous day's close. A lap down occurs when a stock's price opens lower than its previous day's close, but not lower than its previous day's low. A lap up is when a stock's price opens higher than its previous day's close, but not higher than its previous day's high.

Gap Down

Notice on the following chart there is a gap down between the stock's prior daily low and its opening price.

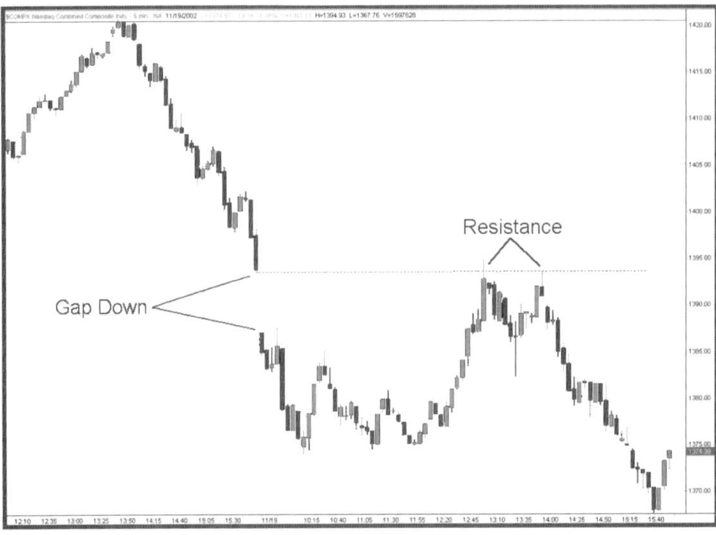

A gap down frequently establishes a level of resistance. In the preceding example, a Double Top test of the gap failed to break through, which confirmed the resistance.

Gap Up

The preceding chart shows a gap up. The stock opened higher than its previous daily high. When a gap up is successfully tested, it becomes support.

Breakaway, Continuation, And Climax Gaps

Occasionally, when support or resistance is particularly strong, it is broken through with a high surge in volume that generates a gap. These types of gaps are frequently the result of a major news event. Regardless of how they occur, they are valid gaps for charting and trading purposes.

Breakaway gaps can occur when a range is broken. *Continuation gaps* occur during an impulsive move, and *climax gaps* occur at the end of a trend. All are generally accompanied by a surge in volume.

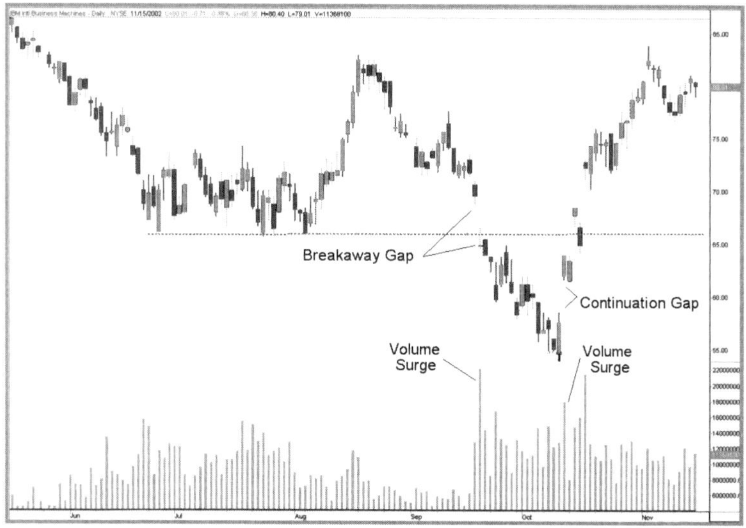

The preceding chart shows a breakaway gap, followed by a continuation gap. Here is a close-up view of the gaps and volume surges.

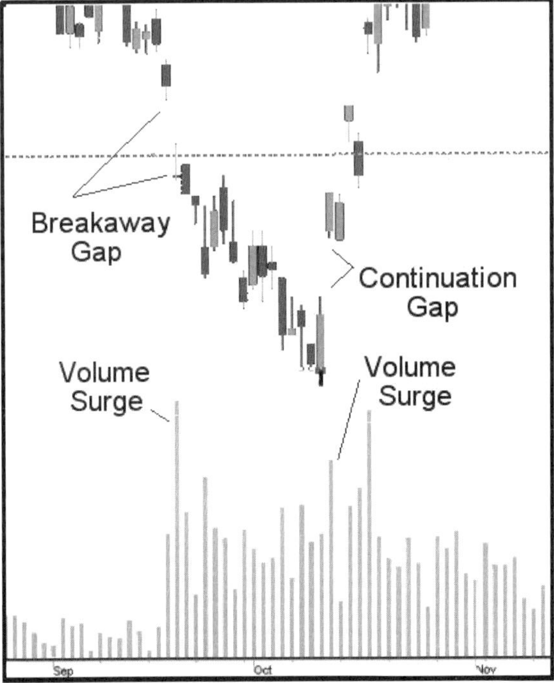

10 - Technical Indicators

What Are Technical Indicators?

In a broad sense, *technical indicators* (or *indicators*) are simply tools that can be analyzed to help predict the future price performance of a stock or the market.

Depending on the options selected, technical indicators appear along with your price chart, typically in an additional panel below the price panel of the chart. A few examples include Volume, Stochastic, RSI, and MACD, but there are many others. Illustrations that show these are provided later.

Technical indicators are generally based on a mathematical formula that uses past price or volume data, or a combination of both. Since the indicators are based primarily on historical data, most of them tend to lag the market.

Even though I use technical indicators regularly to confirm other analysis, I rely mostly on price and volume data. Since many indicators are based on theoretical mathematical formulas, they can be more prone to false signals and misinterpretations. Price and volume is based on actual market data that doesn't lie.

The following sections cover many aspects of technical indicators. An introduction and explanation of many popular indicators, along with their limitations, is covered first. Later, the "Using Momentum Indicators" section provides examples of how you can properly use indicators for additional confirmation of chart patterns.

Should I Use Technical Indicators?

While many of the technical indicators discussed in this chapter can be quite useful, they are not essential and their usage can be somewhat subjective. Depending on your personal preferences and trading style, you might determine indicators are an invaluable resource. However, you might also conclude they are beneficial in specific circumstances only, or that you don't need them at all.

When deciding how to use indicators, the old acronym, K.I.S.S., which stands for "Keep It Simple Stupid", merits consideration. If you master a few analysis tools such as using Flags and Pennants (a couple of my favorite chart patterns), you may discover that you can make a living, or a satisfactory investment return, using only the few tools you've mastered. It's possible that adding more complexity could hinder rather than help your trading. It's not unheard of for successful traders to branch into other areas only to discover the additional complexity compromised a simple moneymaking strategy they already had in place. Where they once had profitable trades consistently, they began losing money. Though indicators can be useful, you may want to keep this in mind when deciding how much to rely on them.

Use Indicators For Confirmation

In general, technical indicators should be used to confirm a chart pattern or a trade setup, and not the other way around. In other words, you shouldn't first look at an indicator then try to find a pattern to justify a trade. Instead, you should first find a pattern setup then see if a given indicator confirms the setup.

For example, suppose you notice that an indicator reflects an *oversold* condition. Having observed this, you might be tempted to look for signs of a bottom in an effort to pick an entry for a trade. This would be using a pattern to confirm an indicator, which is not the proper approach. Instead, once you come across a potential pattern setup, you could check other indicators to see if they also confirm the setup.

There is an exception to the above recommendation. If you do not yet know how to use technical analysis well, then you could use indicators to provide some additional confirmation for a trade.

Regardless of how you use indicators, be aware that there is no such thing as a "perfect" indicator. New indicators come and go frequently, and they are often accompanied with hype about how great they work. Rather than believing the hype outright, a reasonable amount of due diligence is merited.

Overbought & Oversold Conditions

The terms *overbought* and *oversold* may sound familiar. This is because they are used quite frequently in the market. But what do these terms really mean?

Quite simply, when the market or a stock has gone up too far, in too short of a time period, it is considered to be *overbought* and past due for a pullback. Conversely, when the market or a stock has gone down too far, in too short of a time period, it is considered to be *oversold* and is past due to rally. This topic will be covered in more detail in sections that follow.

Momentum Indicators

Momentum is the amount of relative strength or power behind a price movement. It is frequently associated with a surge in volume that is also accompanied by an impulsive price movement.

Momentum is a *leading* technical indicator, meaning it leads the market, which can give you a useful edge by providing advance warning of a potential price move. Since momentum leads, new momentum highs are often followed by new price highs, and new momentum lows are often followed by new price lows.

In an uptrend, when momentum wanes, you may want to consider getting out of long positions, and/or consider whether to enter a short position. When momentum wanes in a downtrend, you may want to consider getting out of short positions, and/or consider whether to enter a long position. This doesn't mean that you should immediately close or enter a position, but you could tighten a stop-loss on an existing position, or watch for other patterns that might indicate a top, bottom, or price reversal. In other words, you shouldn't allow the indicator alone to determine the trade, but you can use it as warning sign or additional confirmation.

Stochastic Indicator

A Stochastic oscillator is a technical indicator that compares a stock's closing price to its price range over a specified period of time. Developed by George Lane, it's one of the most popular momentum oscillators.

Lane theorized that prices tend to close near their highs in a market that is trending up, and prices tend to close near their lows in a market that is trending down. Additionally, as a trend nears its end, prices tend to close a greater distance from their highs or lows, which could indicate the start of a trend reversal.

Although getting into an in-depth discussion of the mathematical calculations involved is beyond the scope of this book, a general overview follows.

Stochastic indicators are plotted using a %K line and a %D line. A calculation that is based upon the highest high-price and the highest low-price plots the %K line. A moving average of the %K plots the %D line. The Stochastic scale ranges from 0 to 100 with 20 or below indicating an oversold condition and 80 or above indicating an overbought condition.

Though most settings will work okay, settings of 14,6,3 for the Stochastic time period, %K, and %D, respectively, are good choices for a daily, slow stochastic. For an intraday Stochastic, you can try 8,3,3 for a slow Stochastic. You can use faster %Ks and %Ds to derive more "signals"; however, you may encounter more swings and a larger number of false signals than with slower settings.

Here is a chart that shows a Stochastic indicator.

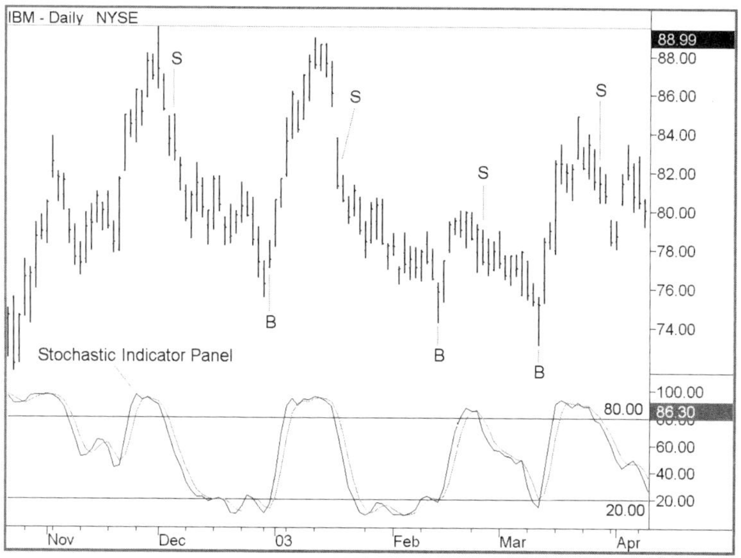

Referring to the previous chart, the traditional use of the Stochastic indicator is as follows. When the Stochastic indicator moves up through 20, it is a buy signal, which is indicated with a B. When the Stochastic indicator moves up through 80 then begins to turn back down, it is a sell signal, which is indicated with an "S".

Although the Stochastic indicator worked great on the preceding chart, it's not always that simple. The Stochastic indicator can also move to an overbought or oversold condition and remain that way for an extended period of time (an example is shown later). Other times, false buy or sell signals may appear.

On the chart above, the traditional approach for using a Stochastic indicator worked reasonably well at first, but look what happened later. If you had acted upon the Stochastic buy signal outlined with a box, you would have lost money on the trade since the price continued down at an even steeper rate. The traditional buy and sell signal would not have worked.

A Stochastic indicator works best when a stock is in a range. If a stock is in a directional trend, the indicator is less reliable. Referring back to the preceding chart, the indicator worked best ahead of the sharp downtrend. Therefore, when a trend is strong, you may want to avoid entering a trade based solely on a Stochastic indicator.

Here's another example.

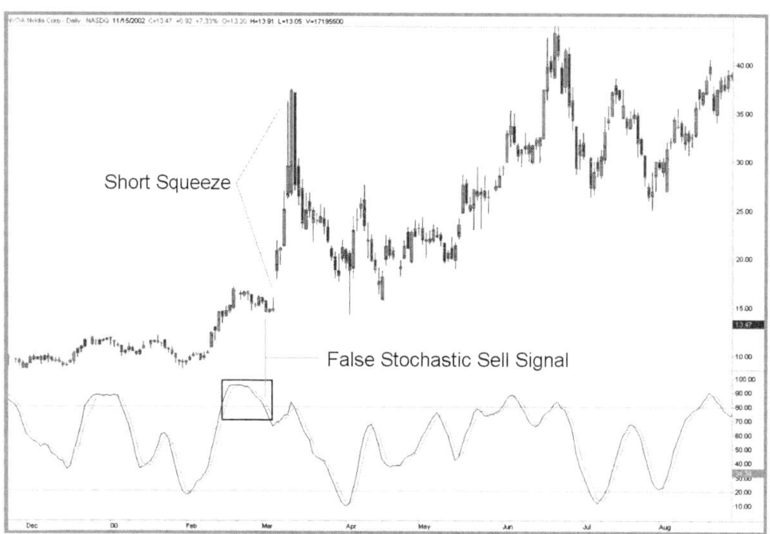

Notice on the preceding chart that it would have been even more problematic to use the Stochastic indicator to time your trades. You might have occasional hits, but you could also have significant misses. Look at the Stochastic sell signal that occurred just ahead of a strong impulsive price move. If you had entered a trade based upon the Stochastic sell signal, you would have entered a short position just before the huge price upswing. Since the upswing began with a gap, you would have taken a significant hit on the trade before having an opportunity to exit your position. And if you had held waiting for a pullback to get out, it would have been much worse.

By using other charting tools rather than relying only on the Stochastic indicator, you would have known to enter a long position rather than short position. The first impulse was a break of a range that was then followed by a Bull Flag, one of the strongest patterns you can trade. You would have known to enter a position long either during the formation of the Bull Flag, or on a breakout of the Flag. You could have subsequently limited your risk by setting a stop-loss order slightly below the bottom of the Flag. See "Flags" in the "Chart Patterns" chapter for more specific information.

The Stochastic indicator can also stay in an oversold or overbought condition for a prolonged period of time. See the following chart.

This chart shows how the Stochastic indicator can stay in an oversold condition. Notice the area within the outlined box. Even though it didn't reach 20 (the actual buy signal), it did start moving higher, which still might have been taken as a buy signal by many traders. The price fell by more 20% after that point. If you were an investor and entered a long position at that point, mistakenly believing the Stochastic had bottomed out, you would have lost a considerable sum of money.

The Stochastic indicator can also stay in a prolonged overbought condition.

Referring to the chart, notice how the Stochastic indicator moved to an overbought condition and remained there for an extended period of time. During this period, if you had taken any downturn as a sell signal to enter a short position, you would have lost money on the trade. However, if you had been fortunate enough to catch the beginning of the move up with a long position as the Stochastic first broke 20, you would have made out great.

RSI Indicator

Welles Wilder, a pioneer in indicator development, invented the RSI indicator, or Relative Strength Index. It is another popular momentum indicator.

Relative strength refers to the internal strength of a stock's price relative to itself and its past performance over a period of time. It's plotted on a scale from 0 to 100, though it's unlikely you'll ever see 0 or 100. Similar to the Stochastic indicator, a value less than 20 indicates an oversold condition and a value over 80 indicates an overbought condition. In a volatile range bound market, you could use 25 and 75 as the parameters.

The time period affects the overall volatility of the indicator, where a shorter time period is more volatile. You can use a standard 14-day time period in most cases (the default for most charting software), and for an intraday setting, you can use 8 for the time period.

The preceding chart shows an RSI indicator. While there were valid buy signals, there were also false signals where the price continued to fall after the RSI indicator crossed above 20. The odds of timing a correct entry for a trade were only about 50/50, so you might as well flip a coin. Obviously, you would want to use other patterns and indicators for additional guidance.

ROC Indicator

The ROC, or Rate Of Change, indicator plots a stock's percentage price change over a specified time period. Or put another way, it displays the percentage difference between a stock's current price and its past prices over a specified rolling-time-period. The ROC indicator is essentially the same as the Momentum indicator, except for differences in scaling.

You can use a setting of 12 for the time period, which is my preference for a daily chart. I don't use the ROC indicator intraday.

Unlike the Stochastic indicator, which uses specific scale values such as 20 or 80 to determine overbought and oversold conditions, the ROC indicator compares the current level to prior levels.

See the following illustration.

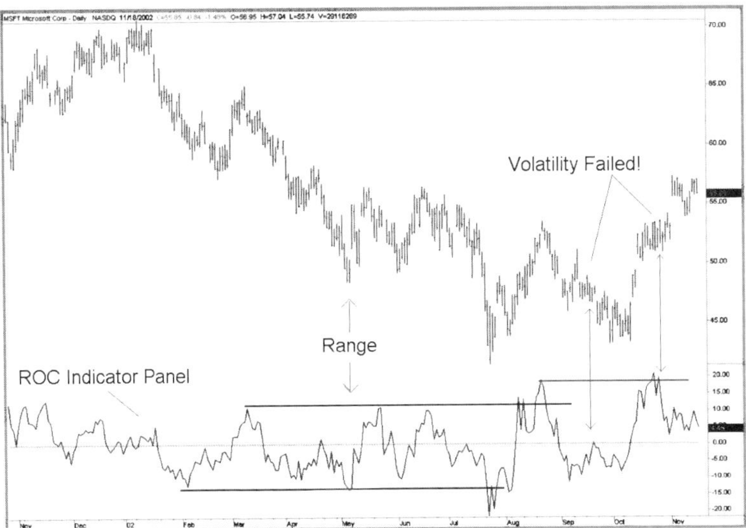

The high points of the ROC indicator signal overbought conditions while the low points of the indicator signal oversold conditions.

As seen on the preceding chart, although it's not perfect, the ROC indicator performs reasonably well when the stock is trading in a range. However, when the price is volatile or is in a strong directional trend, the ROC indicator tends to send more false signals. On the right side of the chart where the price is volatile, notice how the ROC falls while the stock price breaks out. If you had acted upon the ROC sell signal to enter a short position at this point, the trade would have gone against you.

MACD Indicator

Gerald Appel developed the MACD (Moving Average Convergence / Divergence) indicator. MACD is a trend following momentum indicator.

MACD shows the difference between the closing prices of two exponential moving averages, a 26 period moving average and a 12 period moving average. It's applied with a *signal line* that is based on a 9 period exponential moving average. MACD is calculated by dividing one of the moving averages by the other.

A crossover of the signal line indicates a buy or sell signal. A sell signal occurs when the MACD falls below its signal line, and a buy signal occurs when the MACD rises above its signal line.

On the preceding chart, when both lines of the MACD cross above the signal line, a buy signal occurs. Similarly, when both lines cross below the signal line, a sell signal occurs. Notice on the chart that by the time a buy or sell signal takes place, a significant portion of the price move has already been missed. Although the traditional use of the MACD indicator would have worked, you could have caught the price moves sooner using the correct method shown next.

Using Momentum Indicators

As demonstrated in the preceding sections of the book, momentum indicators tend to be prone to false signals. You may be wondering why you should even consider using them at all when they send so many false signals.

Well, taking into consideration their limitations, they can still be very useful to confirm other analysis. You can use them more reliably for confirmation by watching for *Divergence* between the indicator and the price action.

Divergence occurs when the price makes a higher high and the momentum indicator doesn't; or when the price makes a lower low and the indicator doesn't.

Stochastic Divergence

See the following Stochastic chart for an example of divergence. Notice on the chart that when the price makes a high, which is then followed by another comparable high (at the top of the chart), the Stochastic indicator at the bottom also made a high, but it was followed with a lower high. The divergence indicates momentum to the upside is waning, and the price fell a short time later.

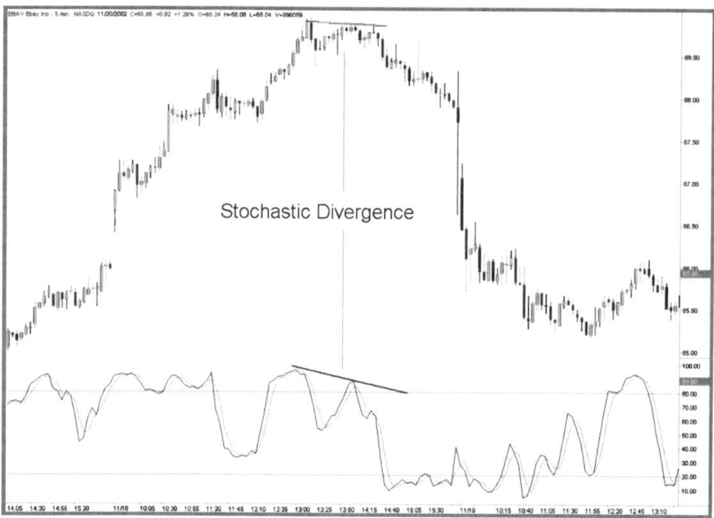

When divergence such as this appears, you should either exit any long position you might have, or tighten your stop-loss order. You could also consider entering a short position. However, waiting for additional price confirmation using the chart patterns described earlier in the book is preferred. Following is another example of divergence.

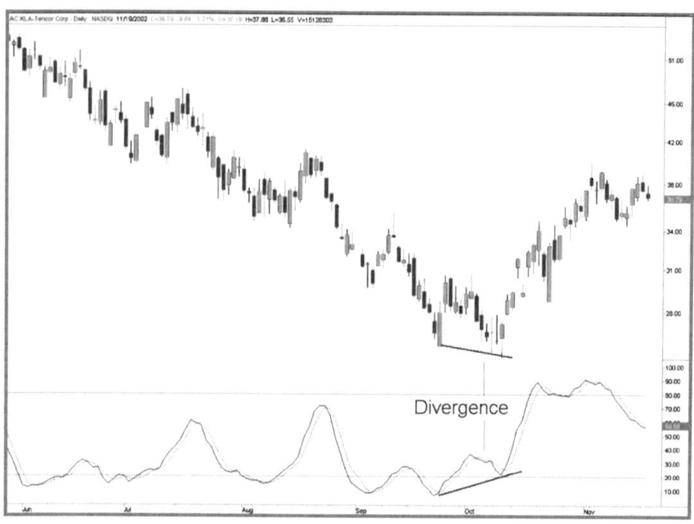

In the preceding example, the divergence is a signal to potentially exit a short position or enter a long position. Notice during the bottoming process, as the price was making lower lows, the Stochastic indicator made a higher low. The divergence signals momentum to the downside is waning. In this case, you should exit any short position you might have, or tighten your stop-loss order on the position. You might also consider entering a long position at this point, or you could wait for additional chart pattern confirmation before entering a long position. Whether to go long here is subject to your own risk tolerance and overall market conditions, but it at least puts a checkmark in the long-side column. Meaning, the Stochastic indicator favors a long trade, if other factors agree.

The preceding chart shows another divergent sell signal. Notice the price pattern is an ascending Triangle, which could indicate a break to the upside. However, the Stochastic indicator isn't confirming. The Stochastic is diverging and making lower highs, indicating momentum is waning. Once again, this would be a signal to watch any long positions carefully, or to wait for additional confirmation before entering a position. In this situation, it's also best to wait for additional price confirmation (a break or retest of the Triangle) before entering a short position.

Another example follows.

This time the price is making a Double Top but the Stochastic is trending down, indicating again that momentum is waning. Look what happens to the price a short time later.

When you see the divergence forming, you would exit any long position or watch it more closely with a stop-loss order just below the base of the Double Top.

You could also consider entering a short position upon a break of the Double Top's base, or at the subsequent Bear Flag that forms after the first impulse to the downside.

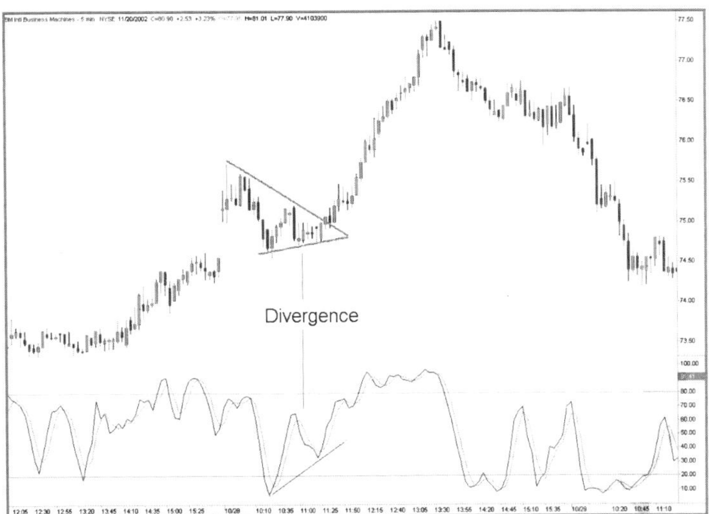

You can also use a Stochastic indicator to watch for divergence with an intraday chart, or to help determine the underlying strength of a move.

Notice on the previous chart, a consolidation phase is forming a Triangle pattern. Since the Triangle is preceded by an impulsive move up, a continuation of the move with a breakout of the Triangle to the upside is anticipated. Looking at the Stochastic indicator, you'll see it is making higher lows during the formation of the Triangle, which indicates the upside momentum is increasing. Instead of a divergence, there is a convergence. You now have two indicators signaling a continuation of the move to the upside.

Since the Stochastic indicator also confirmed a move to the upside, you could enter a long position during the consolidation of the Triangle and define your risk with a stop-loss order slightly below the lower trendline of the Triangle. However, keep in mind that the risk is higher with this setup. You should only trade it if you don't mind getting stopped out of your position should the trade go against you. If you don't like the idea of getting stopped-out, then aggressive entries such as this, even those based upon technical analysis, are *not* for you. It's also important to know yourself before making the trade.

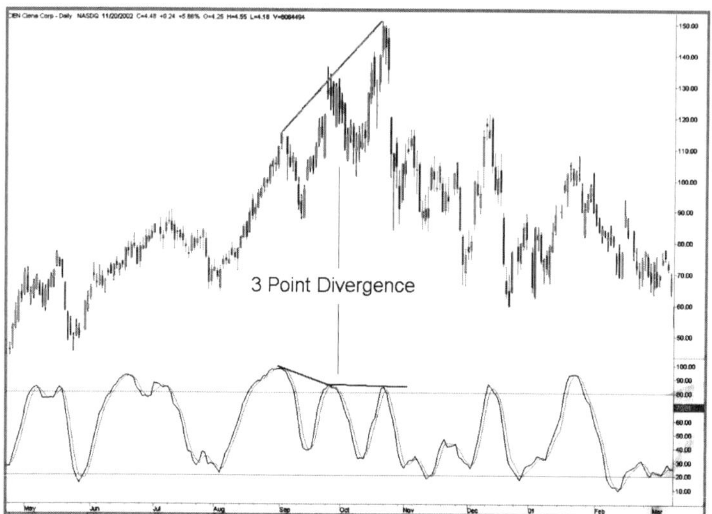

The preceding chart is interesting because it not only illustrates a 3-point divergence; it shows a climatic end to a trend. Often a trend will end with three pushes to a climax, that is, three pushes to a top, or three pushes to a bottom. See the area indicated with an ascending trendline that shows three pushes to a climatic top.

While the price is rising, notice the divergence that is taking place on the Stochastic indicator. There is a divergence between the first two swing high points, and another divergence between the second two swing high points. This is a 3-point divergence. If you had entered a short position after the first divergence, you would have probably had a small gain, assuming you stopped out or covered your position before the next push up. But, if you had managed to get in after the second divergence, you would have done particularly well, having caught the large downside impulse.

RSI Divergence

You can also use divergence on an RSI indicator for additional confirmation of a chart pattern. You'll need to look closely on the following chart because the divergence is a bit subtler, but it is present.

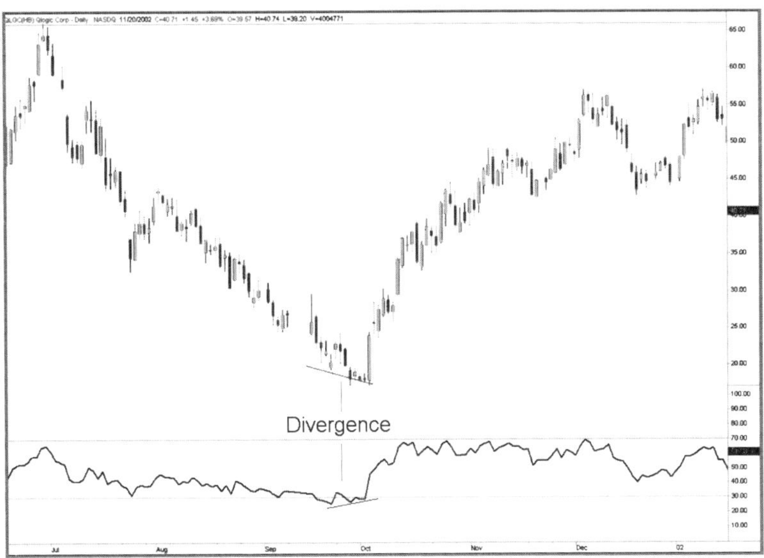

On the chart at the point where the price is lowest, just before the impulsive upswing, the RSI indicator made a slightly higher low.

While the divergence is tight, it did signal the trend reversal. The price made a lower low, and the RSI indicator made a higher low. Is this a strong enough signal to enter long position? Maybe not, but it is enough to warrant a protective stance on a short position.

Another example that shows a wider RSI Divergence follows.

Notice the divergence that takes place where the trendlines are drawn. The price made a lower low, while the RSI indicator made a higher low.

ROC Divergence

In most cases, divergences of the ROC indicator resemble RSI divergences. However, for illustration purposes, an example follows that shows a different type of divergence.

Notice that a short ROC divergence first appeared as the price moved to a new high. Afterwards, the price repeatedly retested the high, but the ROC indicator fell off a cliff then continued to trend downward, which resulted in another long divergence. After the ROC indicator made the initial two high points at the first divergence, it failed to even get close to those high levels again, even though the price was continuing to retest its high. Since the upside momentum completely disappeared, the ROC divergence was a signal that the price range could breakdown, which it subsequently did.

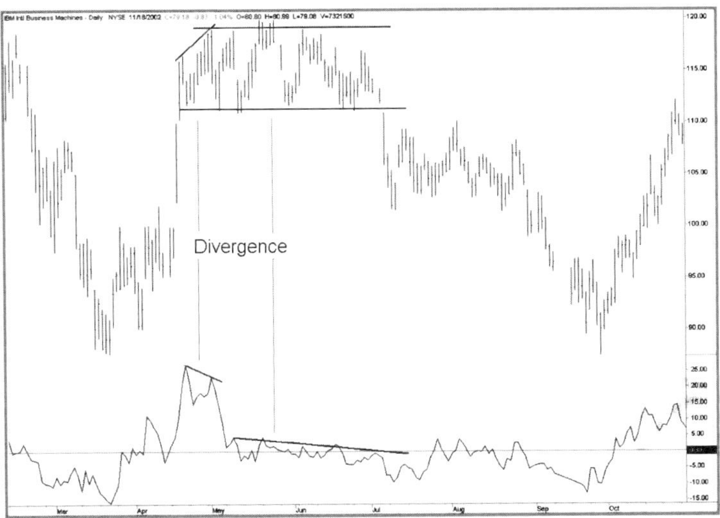

MACD Divergence

You can use also use divergences of the MACD indicator as confirmation.

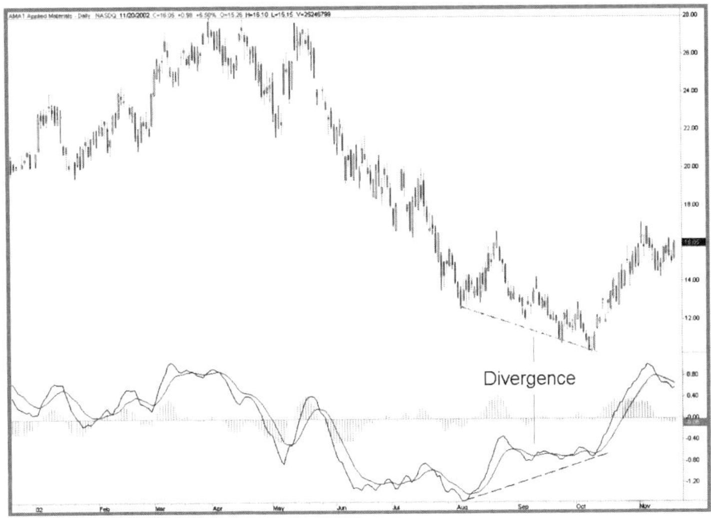

See the preceding chart for a very noticeable divergence of the MACD indicator. While the price is making lower lows, the MACD indicator is making higher lows, indicating the downtrend momentum is falling off. Subsequently, the downtrend breaks with an impulsive move to the upside.

This is another example of a 3-point divergence. Notice the three lower price-lows that correspond to the three higher MACD lows. In this case, the divergence corresponds to three pushes to a bottom.

Volume Indicators

As you may recall from earlier chapters, volume indicates the amount of interest or "crowd participation" in a stock. You can also use volume to determine whether a stock is being accumulated or distributed.

Accumulation occurs when the price of a stock closes higher, and on higher volume, than it did on the prior day. Distribution occurs when the price of a stock closes lower, but on higher volume, than it did the prior day.

When using volume, the standard volume histogram panel works best. You may also find it useful to overlay the volume's moving average. This lets you easily spot volume trends or see when volume spikes or valleys deviate from the average.

Even though the standard volume panel is my preference for general use, there are other volume indicators you may find useful. Some are based on relationships between price and volume.

On Balance Volume (OBV)

Joe Granville developed *On Balance Volum*e, or OBV, a volume indicator that is based on the relationship between a stock's volume and its price over a period of time.

OBV is an accumulated total that is calculated by adding closing volumes to the total volume when prices close up, and subtracting them from the total when prices close down. The result is an accumulative total that indicates whether overall volume is flowing into or out of a stock over a specified time period. Therefore, it indicates whether a stock is being accumulated or distributed. Since volume will often lead price, OBV can be a leading indicator.

The following chart shows an OBV indicator. Notice on the chart that as the stock price rises, the OBV indicator also rises, which confirms the stock is being accumulated.

Later, the OBV indicator begins to fall off and takes out a prior low, which means more caution is appropriate. If you are long, you might want to tighten your stop-loss order at this point. The next chart shows a case where the OBV indicator does not confirm the price move.

The OBV indicator is essentially moving sideways rather than moving higher in conjunction with the price. Notice the upward price momentum isn't sustained and both the price and OBV indicator subsequently fall.

Volatility Indicators

Volatility is a measure of how much a stock's price fluctuates over a period of time. For example, if a stock has large price swings over a relatively short period of time, it is considered to be more volatile than if the price changes very little.

There has been extensive research over the years into volatility and the market. One of the strongest findings is that volatility is *mean reverting*. This means that periods of low volatility are followed by periods of high volatility and vice versa, which can be of great help in analyzing stocks and the overall market.

ADX Indicator

Welles Wilder developed the *directional movement index*, referred to as the ADX. The ADX is one of my favorite indicators. It measures the strength of a trend, but not a trend's direction.

Since the ADX is a volatility indicator, low readings indicate low volatility, which are signs of an impending move. Low readings mean the market is quiet, which often leads to explosive moves.

High readings signal the market may be getting overextended. In this case, you may want to tighten stop-loss orders and watch for a possible reversal.

The ADX scale ranges from 0 to 100. The values do not indicate direction. They only indicate whether the market, or a stock, is range bound or in a strong trend. You can use a 14 period ADX for setting all timeframes including daily and intraday (5-minute and above).

A value below 10 indicates volatility is very low. This is a time to watch closely for a move. Values above 30 indicate a strong market trend. If the ADX goes above 50, I automatically tighten my trailing stop-loss order by cutting it in half, since the trend is showing signs of becoming overextended. And, if the ADX goes above 80, I exit the trade as it indicates the trend is substantially overextended.

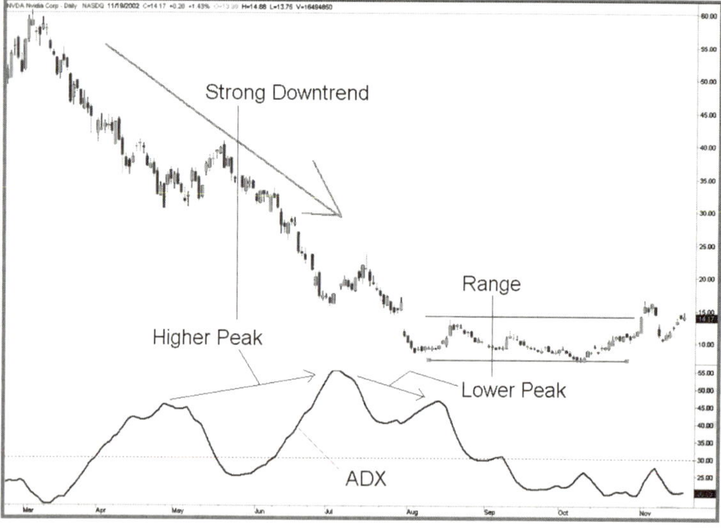

Notice that during the strong downtrend on the preceding chart, the ADX indicator is above 30 reflecting the strong trend. When the ADX peaks (your stop-loss should be tightened by this point), the downtrend is about to begin a transition into a range bound trend, and the ADX drops accordingly.

As long as the ADX continues to make higher peaks, you can continue to play the trend. However, once the ADX makes a lower peak, it indicates the trend is losing momentum and a range could be beginning. Therefore, it's time to stop playing the trend. Notice the correlation between the narrow sideways price range and the ADX indicator on the previous chart. After the ADX highs, the next lower ADX peak coincides with the transition into a range bound price trend.

The ADX indicator can also be used to help confirm a Triangle chart pattern.

Since a Triangle is a period of consolidation, you would expect to see a nice low ADX indicator.

Referring to the prior chart, you'll see an example of this. Once the Triangle breaks to the downside, you could enter a short position (see the chapter on chart patterns for more detailed information about Triangles and other patterns).

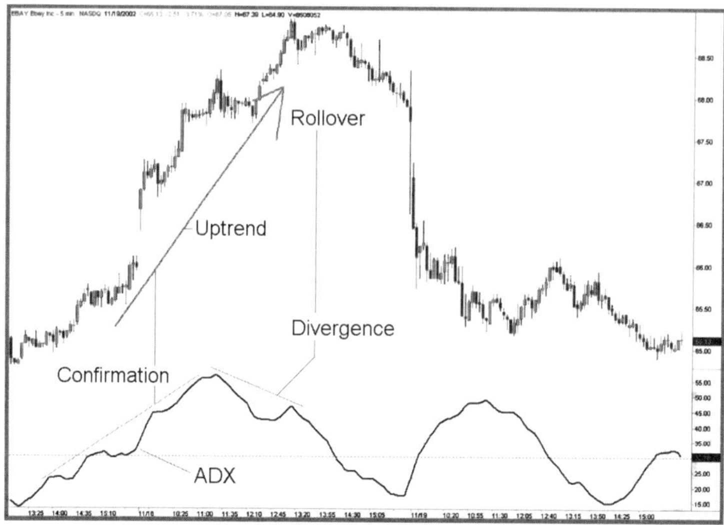

The above chart shows how you can use the ADX indicator to confirm intraday trends. Notice how the ADX confirmed the strong uptrend. Later, there was an ADX divergence near the price top followed by a lower ADX high, signaling an overextended trend, which did subsequently rollover.

Bolinger Bands

John Bolinger invented Bolinger Bands, an indicator that is plotted as two lines, or bands, at standard deviations above and below a moving average.

The bands expand in volatile time periods and contract in calmer periods. Some additional characteristics of Bollinger Bands are:

- Tight, or narrow, bands tend to lead to impulsive price moves.
- Many analysts believe prices that approach or cross the upper band indicate an overbought condition, and prices that approach or cross the lower band indicate an oversold condition, which could lead to reversals.

- Prices that move outside the bands tend to result in trend continuations; however, price tops and bottoms that occur outside of the bands, which are followed by tops and bottoms that occur inside the bands, tend to lead to trend reversals.
- Prices that start at one band tend to move to the other band, which may be useful as a tool for projecting price targets.

For chart settings, you can try 20,2,2 for daily charts, and 13,2,2 for intraday charts, where the first number is the time period followed by the up and down deviation parameters.

A chart with Bollinger Bands follows.

On the preceding chart, the centerline shows the Bollinger moving average. Above and below the moving average, you'll see two lines that represent the Bollinger Bands. Notice that each time the price crossed either of the Bollinger Bands, it tended to pull back within the bands.

The method for trading Bollinger Bands varies among traders and is subject to your own experience and preferences. I don't use Bollinger Bands extensively. Rather than basing trade entries on price moves outside of the bands, I "occasionally" use them as additional confirmation of overbought or oversold conditions, and in conjunction with my other analysis, consider whether to exit a trade, tighten my stops, or watch a position more closely.

At times, I also find Bollinger's useful for signaling potential trend reversals, and for projecting price targets. One of the characteristics listed above was that once a price moves to or beyond a band, it tends to swing back to the other band, so you can use the opposite band as a guideline for setting a potential price target. Looking at the prior chart again, you might have observed that when prices cross the Bollinger Bands, this frequently coincides with impulsive price moves as well, which are also tradable using other techniques that are described earlier in this book. Here's another example Bollinger Bands chart.

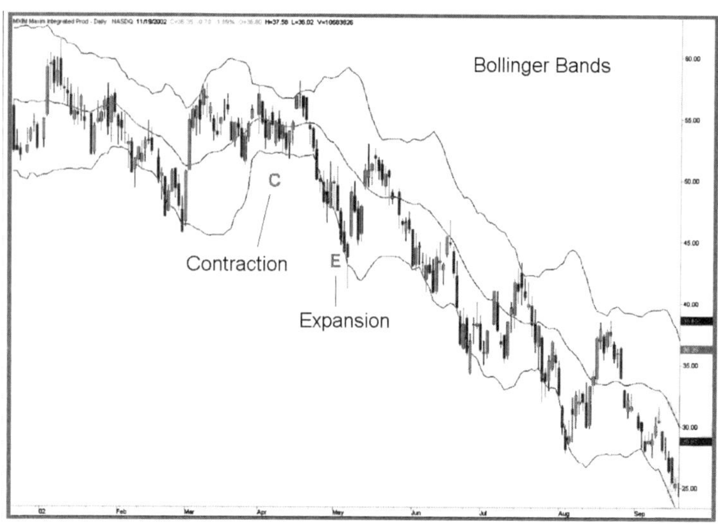

The previous example shows how Bollinger Bands expand and contract. Prices are more volatile when the bands expand and are less volatile when they contract. Notice also that the price is initially in a range then at point C the bands contract. One characteristic of contracting bands is that it tends to lead a sharp price change, as is demonstrated by the next impulse to the downside with an associated expansion of the Bollinger Bands at point E.

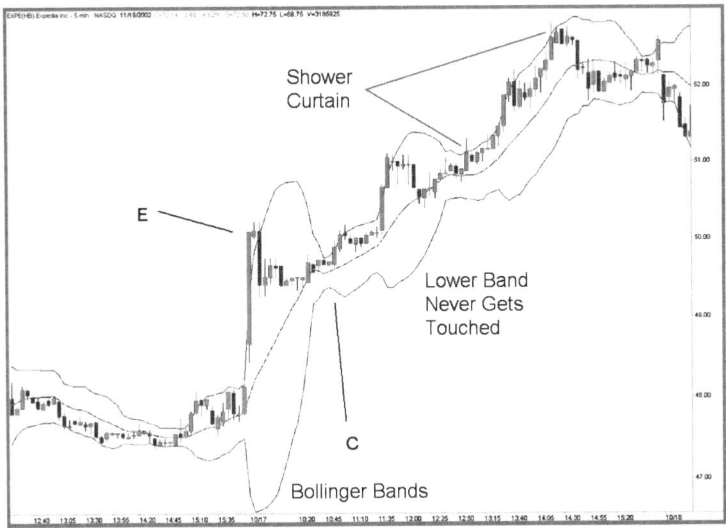

The above intraday Bollinger chart shows a very strong uptrend. Notice how the price runs right up the upper band during the latter part of the trend. This is sometimes referred to as a *shower curtain.*

Like with all technical indicators, Bollinger Bands are not perfect. One of the implied characteristics of Bollinger Bands is that if the price crosses one of the bands, it tends to move back to the opposite band. However, as can be seen on the preceding chart at points E, C and thereafter, there are numerous instances where a trade wouldn't have worked if you had entered a short position when the price crossed the upper band. The price didn't fall back to the price targets at the lower band. Therefore, as with all indicators, you should use Bollinger Bands in conjunction with other analysis methods (chart patterns, Japanese candlesticks, etc.).

Historical Volatility Ratio

Historical volatility is the fluctuation of a stock's past volatility over a period of time. The *Historical Volatility Ratio* (HV Ratio) is a ratio between the 6-day and 100-day historical volatility.

When the HV Ratio dips below 0.5, meaning volatility is getting very low; it's time to watch for a potential expansion move since volatility tends to revert back to its mean, or average historical level.

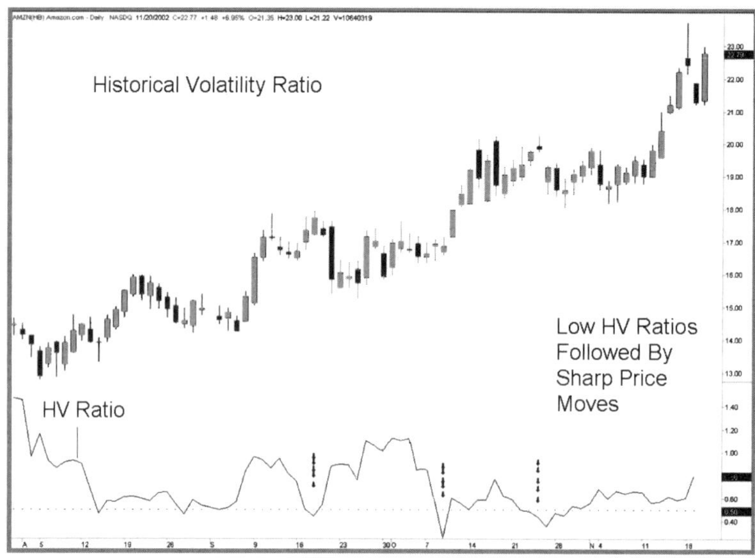

On the preceding chart, notice that each time the price entered a range and the HV Ratio was correspondingly low, there was a subsequent impulsive move to the upside. The low HV Ratio levels confirmed the range and consolidation periods where there was little interest in the stock. Each time, it was followed by a sharp price move and increase in volatility.

Following is another HV Ratio example.

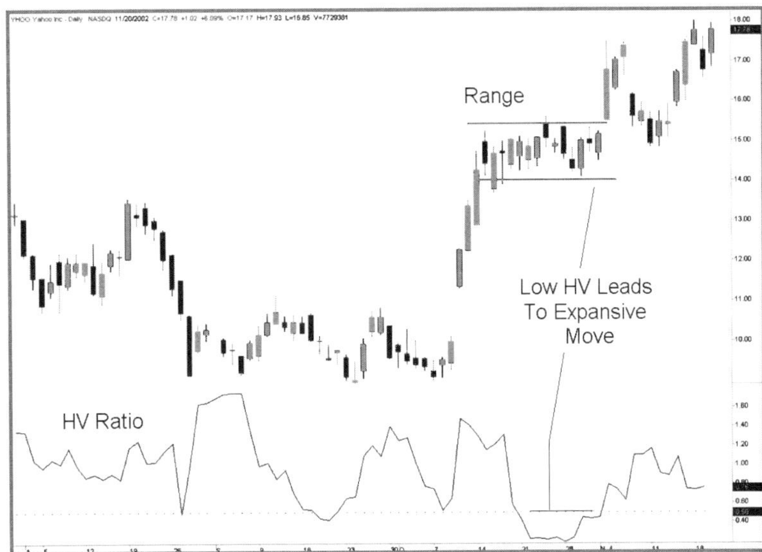

Notice the range bracketed by the trendlines, and the corresponding low HV indicator, which is then followed by an expansive breakout to the upside.

Though I don't use the HV Ratio for intraday trades, I think it's a good intermediate term indicator. However, keep in mind that the HV Ratio is like the ADX indicator. It does not predict direction, just that a movement is coming.

11 - Fibonacci Analysis

Fibonacci analysis is based on ratios derived from the famous Fibonacci Series of numbers, which were discovered by a 13th century mathematician named Leonardo Fibonacci.

Beginning with 0 and 1, each subsequent number in the Fibonacci Series is produced by adding together the two previous numbers in the series. The result is a series of numbers such as 0, 1, 1, 2, 3, 5, 8, 13, 21, 34, 55, 89, which continues on to infinity.

A golden mean ratio of .618 is derived from dividing 55 by 89 at the eighth series. Another commonly used ratio is its inverse of 1.618, which is 89 divided by 55. These ratios, and others based upon them, are found frequently in nature. Stock market analysts often use them to predict potential levels of support and resistance.

When a trend or price swing comes to an end, Fibonacci ratios are often used to predict where a subsequent retracement may encounter support or resistance. Common Fibonacci support and resistance percentages are used for this purpose. *Internal* retracement percentages are used on the inside of market swings and *extensions*, or *external*, retracement percentages are used on the outside, which is when a retracement exceeds the length of the original swing. Examples of each type are provided later.

Following are the commonly used Fibonacci retracement percentages, which you will likely want to retain for future reference. They are used extensively for plotting Fibonacci grids (explained later) to determine potential support and resistance levels during price retracements.

Internal Fibonacci retracement percentages:

38.2%, 50%, 61.8%, 78.6%, 100%

Note: 70.7% is sometimes used as well.

Extensions, or external, Fibonacci percentages:

127.2%, 141.4%, and 161.8%

For convenience, the numbers are frequently rounded to the nearest whole number (e.g., 38%, 62%, etc.). There are other retracement percentages that you may read about elsewhere, but these are the numbers I use and feel work the best.

Fibonacci Grid

You plot a Fibonacci grid by connecting the two most recent distant points of a swing (the most recent lowest swing low to the most recent highest swing high, or vise-versa). Then, you use the Fibonacci percentages previously provided to determine potential levels of support and resistance. See the following example.

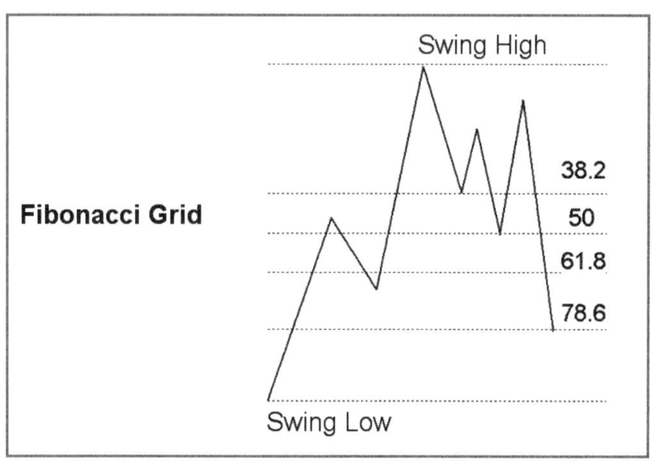

Note that most of the good charting software lets you draw a line from a swing low to a swing high then it plots the Fibonacci grid for you automatically, so you don't have to be a math wiz or keep a calculator handy to use a Fibonacci grid.

As always, confirmation is key when using Fibonacci support and resistance levels.

Fibonacci Retracements

An example of a Fibonacci retracement follows.

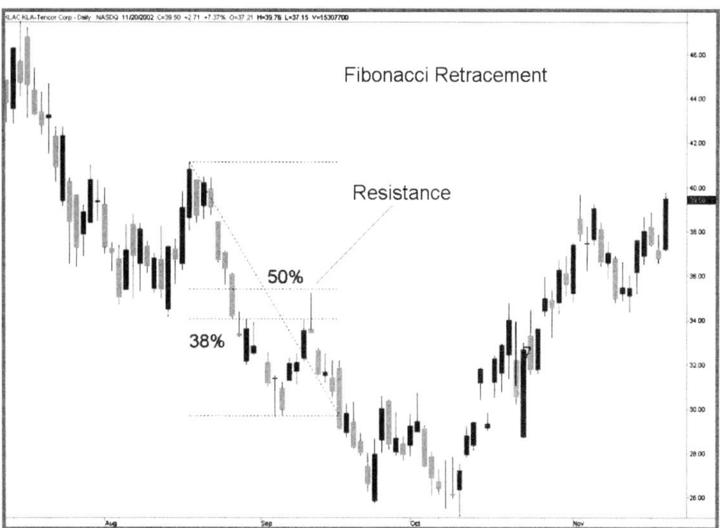

Notice on the preceding chart after the large swing to the downside, a retracement to the 38% Fibonacci resistance level failed a retest. However, a subsequent retracement to the 50% Fibonacci resistance held.

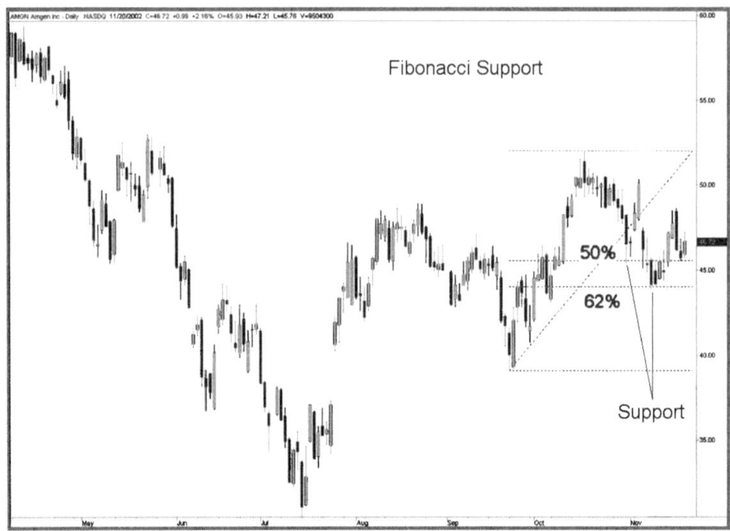

The chart above shows an example of Fibonacci support using a swing to the upside. The first retracement bounced at the 50% Fibonacci support level. On the next retracement the 50% Fibonacci breaks down but the 61.8% Fibonacci holds.

Once again, you want to look for confirmation of the Fibonacci support or resistance levels before relying upon them.

Occasionally, multiple indicators of support or resistance line up with one another. When this occurs, it creates even stronger levels of support and resistance. And the more Fibonacci grid lines or other indicators that line up, the more likely the support or resistance will hold. An example of this is shown on the next chart.

The price is range bound at the beginning of the following chart then breaks out with an impulsive move to the upside. You can create a Fibonacci grid from the swing low of the range to the high of the impulsive move up.

The subsequent retracement tested both the 38% Fibonacci and a gap that occurred during the impulse. The pullback filled the gap. Additionally, you might have noticed the Doji candle on the chart, which is also indicative of a reversal.

Though it is beyond the scope of this book, it is possible to lay additional Fibonacci grids on top of one another based upon subsequent swings, swings inside one another, and so on. This could result in additional overlapping grid lines that highlight even stronger areas of support and resistance.

Fibonacci Extensions

A rule of thumb to keep in mind is that once a retracement breaks the 78.6% Fibonacci level, a retracement back to the 100% Fibonacci is probable. A 100% retracement is actually just a retest of the original swing low or swing high point that you used to define the grid (i.e., a retest of the grid's starting point).

Fibonacci extensions come into play when a retracement exceeds the 100% Fibonacci. These are also referred to as external retracements, since they extend beyond the original swing upon which the Fibonacci was based.

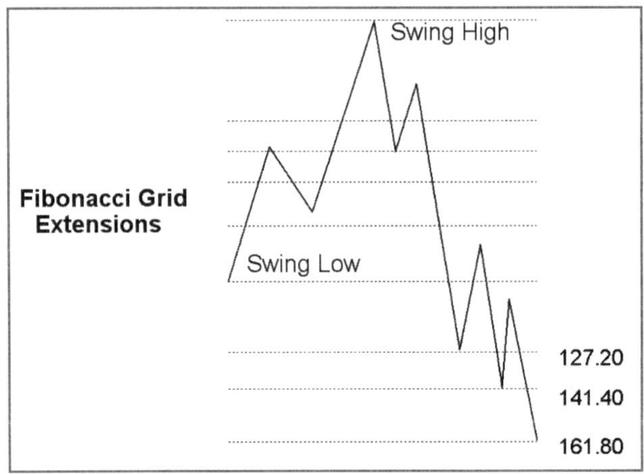

In addition to determining potential levels of support and resistance, Fibonacci extensions are also useful for determining potential lows, highs, or the end of swings.

On the preceding chart, an impulsive move up could potentially break the downtrend. See the swing high that was established at the upper Fibonacci line.

A subsequent swing low bounced off of the 127.2% Fibonacci extension support. Finally, the next impulsive move up does break through the prior swing high resistance, breaking the downtrend.

In this case, the 127.2% Fibonacci correctly marked the swing low from which the price bounced.

On the following chart, the Fibonacci grid is based upon the swing from point A to B and marks a potential level of resistance.

Notice the 127.2% Fibonacci extension resistance at point C holds. In this case, the preceding gap also reinforces and strengthens the resistance.

Fibonacci support and resistance levels can also be used on intraday charts. Notice the upswing that occurs after the gap retraces back to the 141.4% Fibonacci support level on the prior chart.

12 - Inside, Outside And Narrow Range Bars

As previously discussed, stock prices cycle through range and directional trending phases. You can shorten, or narrow, price cycles even further and achieve greater precision by identifying *inside bars*, *outside bars*, and *narrow range bars* on charts.

In general, prices tend to cycle through contraction and expansion phases between inside, outside, and narrow range bars. As with some of the previously discussed chart patterns, these are very powerful trading tools. While they can be used with any timeframe, my preference is to use them on daily charts to help find trading candidates for the next session.

Inside Bars

An inside bar's range is 'inside' the range of the preceding bar. It is defined as follows:

- An inside bar's high is lower than the prior bar's high.
- An inside bar's low is higher than the previous bar's low.

See the following chart for examples of inside bar days.

Notice on the chart that range contraction occurs during the inside bar phase (the price range narrows), which is then followed by range expansion (the price range widens).

The direction of the expansion can be to the downside or upside. Inside bars do not predict direction; they only indicate periods of contraction and expansion. And, similar to volatility, periods of contraction and expansion tend to revert back to their *mean*. When in a contraction, the tendency is toward expansion, and vise versa.

Inside bars are powerful indicators for potential Triangle pattern breakouts. If you see an inside bar about 2/3 of the way through a Triangle (not at the Apex), a breakout is likely to occur soon.

Outside Bars

An outside bar's range is *outside* the range of the preceding bar. Outside bars are an indication of increased volatility.

They often signal a trend reversal when they occur after a prolonged uptrend or downtrend. An outside bar is defined as follows:

- An outside bar's high is higher than the prior bar's high.
- An outside bar's low is lower than the previous bar's low.

Here is an outside bar example.

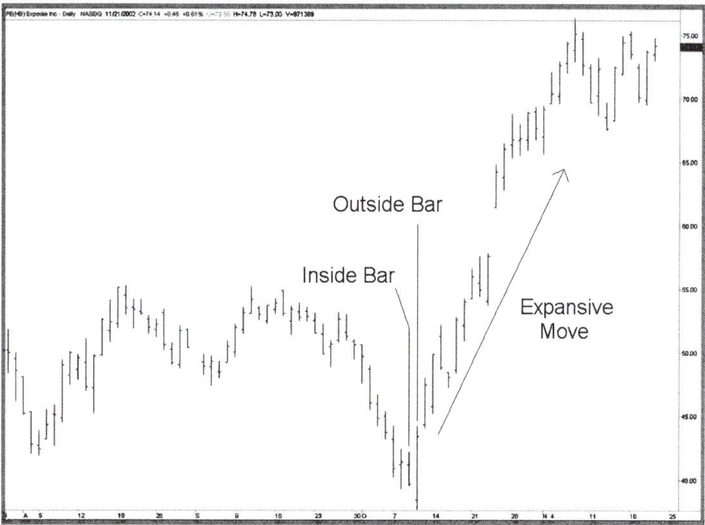

Referring to the previous illustration, near the center of the chart you'll see an inside bar, which is followed by an outside bar. The outside bar signaled a reversal with a large expansive upside move.

Narrow Range Bars

A *narrow range bar* indicates a period of price range contraction and consolidation with low volatility. It tends to occur toward the end of a set period of contraction. A narrow range bar does not need to be an inside or outside bar; it can simply be a narrow range bar.

Following is an example of narrow range bars.

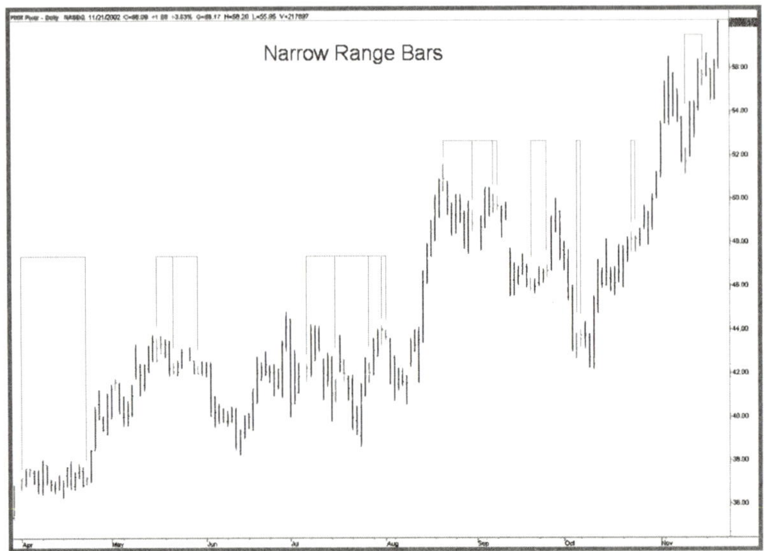

When a narrow range bar occurs at the end of a pullback, it tends to indicate a continuation of the prior trend is likely, so it is usually followed by price range expansion. For example, when an uptrend pulls back and a narrow range bar appears, the uptrend is likely to continue afterwards. A narrow range bar can also signal a breakout or range expansion when it appears near the end of a Flag pattern or when it appears about 2/3 of the way through a Triangle pattern.

Back-to-back inside bars, outside bars, or narrow range bars, or a narrow range bar in combination with either of the other two, tend to be even more powerful. Double-signals often lead to more powerful range expansion (see the previous outside bar chart for an example).

I prefer to see a seven-day narrow range time period, and longer time periods can produce even more powerful results.

13 - Analyzing Trades

Now that you've learned something about charting and technical analysis, it's time to put it to use.

As you likely know by now, there is a virtual plethora of analysis tools available for ferreting out trade setups. Though this book covers a broad spectrum of these tools, there is more available than can be covered thoroughly by any single book such as this, so I encourage you to also seek out additional sources of information and continue to learn.

The possibilities for using such a wealth of analysis tools are limited only by your imagination, and the best approach for analyzing trades varies depending on your trading objectives and personal preferences. To help get you started, this chapter walks you through the process of analyzing a couple of trades using many of the tools and methods introduced throughout this book. However, you shouldn't limit yourself only to the approaches presented here. Feel free to experiment and explore other approaches. Over time, you can develop a personalized approach that works best for you and takes into account your own trading objectives.

Okay, let's get started. What stock should you trade? The process for choosing a specific stock varies widely among traders. Ideally, you'll want to find a *momentum* stock that has plenty of liquidity (volume) so you can get in and out of a trade quickly and easily. You could look for one that is getting attention because it has good or bad earnings expectations, it's in an industry that's hot at the moment, or there is some other breaking news event. If you are already familiar with trading, you can choose among your own favorites or whatever daytrading stocks are popular at the time of this reading. And though it's beyond the scope of this book, another option is to use stock screening software that lets you search for stocks based on a large variety of fundamental and technical criteria including price, volume, market capitalization, and much more.

A word of caution, however, rumors and hype are widespread on the Internet so you should use discretion and independently verify any information obtained online to your own satisfaction, or use only reputable, trusted sources of information such as Trendfund.com.

For illustration purposes, I'm going to pick a couple of momentum stocks at random. My choices are based on whether their current charts show the desired chart patterns and trade setups, not because I have a preference for any particular stock. The processes described could just as easily be applied to any stock.

Analysis 1

After some investigation, I found a stock that has had a very strong upside move and as a result, it could be past due for a pullback. It looks like a good candidate for a possible trade, so let's begin the analysis.

The first step is to take a look at what has happened up to this point. On the following chart, you'll see a strong downtrend that ends with a Double Bottom pattern, which is then followed by signs of impulsive buying. This indicates the downtrend is potentially changing. Notice the subsequent gaps and long-range bars, all of which indicate buyers are lining up. Actually, it looks like they were *chomping at the bit* and couldn't wait to get in.

The upside move is so strong that within a month the stock has gained 50% or more before forming a Topping Shadow. See the Spinning Top candle at point A on the chart, which is also followed by a Doji.

Since the stock price has moved so far in such a relatively short period of time, it is now showing signs of being top heavy. A little further investigation reveals that its industry, the semiconductors, and the Nasdaq technology market overall are also looking overbought.

As you may recall, an overbought condition occurs when prices move too far, too fast, causing a stock to be past due for a pullback. However, also keep in mind that trends have a much better chance of continuing than reversing. Therefore, you don't want to just arbitrarily jump in and start shorting a Topping Shadow. Instead, further analysis and confirmation is desired.

So, a Stochastic indicator is added to the chart. I used settings of 14,6,3.

As you may recall, you don't use an indicator to justify a chart pattern or trade, but rather, you use it for confirmation.

In this case, you can see the Stochastic does confirm an overbought condition, and it has just begun a downward direction.

With the additional confirmation, it's time to start watching for a chart pattern that sets up an entry for a short position. The goal is to make 1 or 2 points on a potential pullback, then see if the original uptrend resumes.

A Fibonacci grid is added to the chart.

Notice a swing low occurs on the preceding chart, which is then followed by a bounce. The bounce moves up to the 78.6% Fibonacci retracement level, an area where resistance could be encountered. This alone still doesn't justify entering a short position. Instead, a more in-depth look is needed.

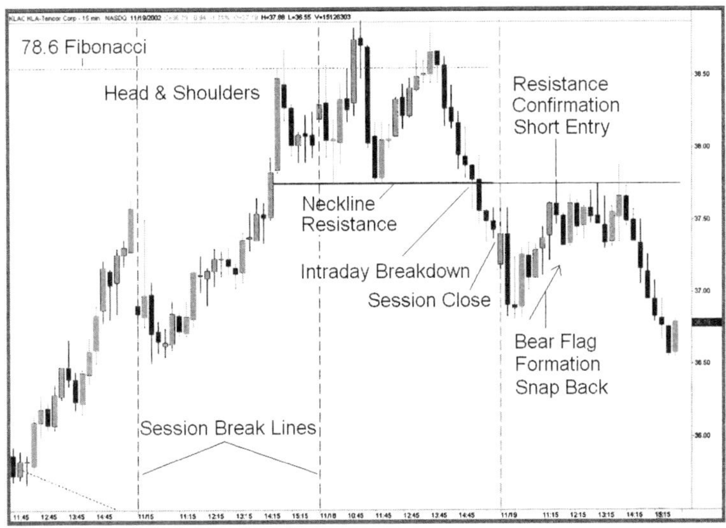

Up to this point, the analysis has used daily charts. Now, it's time to dial down to an intraday chart and see if any additional indicators show up.

On the preceding intraday chart, a Head & Shoulders pattern appears. I added the upper dotted horizontal line to the chart for reference. It is a carryover of the 78.6% Fibonacci retracement (the resistance level) from the prior daily chart. The dashed vertical reference lines simply mark the end-of-day session breaks.

Keep in mind that a break of support or resistance occurs only if the price "closes" above the support or below the resistance, which means the Fibonacci resistance has officially held even though it may have been crossed briefly during intraday trading. Instead of breaking through resistance, the price broke through support at the neckline of the Head & Shoulders, since the price closed the session below the neckline (see the "Session Close" candle at the session break line on the chart).

Still, rather than simply shorting a breakdown of the Head & Shoulders neckline, it is now time to look for confirmation of the breakdown. Recalling one of the characteristics of a Head & Shoulders pattern is a snapback to the neckline, a subsequent snapback is anticipated. And since old support becomes new resistance, resistance is expected at the neckline. Notice on the preceding chart that a swing low is put in after the neckline breakdown, a snapback does occur as expected, and a Bear Flag forms.

The Trade

Finally, it's time to enter the trade. Once the neckline resistance is confirmed (i.e., it is held), you would enter a short position and set a stop-loss order slightly above the top of the Head & Shoulders. In this case, you might have been *grinding your teeth* a bit as the neckline resistance was retested but a continuation of the downward move resumes, which ultimately results in a successful countertrend trade.

Keeping in mind that the original plan was to make 1 or 2 points on the trade, you would exit the trade and take profits accordingly. You could take all of your profits and completely exit your position, or if you have a strong feeling there is more downside momentum, you could take profits on one-half of your position and move your stop-loss order to breakeven on the rest. Afterwards, you would trail any further move to the downside by using an automatic trailing stop-loss order (if supported by your brokerage firm), or by manually adjusting your stop-loss order as the price moves. When the price eventually reverses direction, you will stop out with additional profits, or at the very least, you will stop out at the breakeven point and preserve the profits you previously took on the other half of your position (note that breakeven should also allow for commission costs).

Well, we made out like a bandit on that one (can you see me smiling). Now it's time to find another trade.

Analysis 2

I no sooner start looking and like magic, another great trading opportunity pops up. If only it were that easy! In reality, a lot of hard work, time, and experience are involved.

A chart of the potential trade follows.

Looking at the chart, you'll see a strong impulse to the upside along the right edge. If you look closely, you can also see that an Inverted Head & Shoulders preceded the impulse. A good long entry would have been to play the breakout above the Inverted Head & Shoulders neckline. However, since we missed it, we'll look for another opportunity to trade the breakout.

One of the most powerful trading opportunities occurs during the first pullback after an impulse, during the consolidation period. This can be in the form of a Flag, Pennant, other pattern, or just a straight pullback only. So with that in mind, we start watching for a trading setup.

A Fibonacci grid is added to the chart.

The Fibonacci grid is plotted from the most recent lowest low to the highest high, which is from the bottom of the Inverted Head & Shoulders to the to the swing high after the impulse.

Notice that the stock has retraced to the 38% Fibonacci support level.

If you examine the preceding chart further, you'll see an earlier swing point high that was also near the 38.2% Fibonacci support level (the prior highest high near the center of the chart). This high was prior resistance until the impulsive upside move broke through it. Since old resistance becomes new support, this also creates another potential level of support. As a result, there are now two indicators of support, the prior swing point high, and the 38% Fibonacci.

Next, the key moving averages are added to the chart.

I used the 10, 50, and 200-day simple moving averages, and the 20-day exponential moving average.

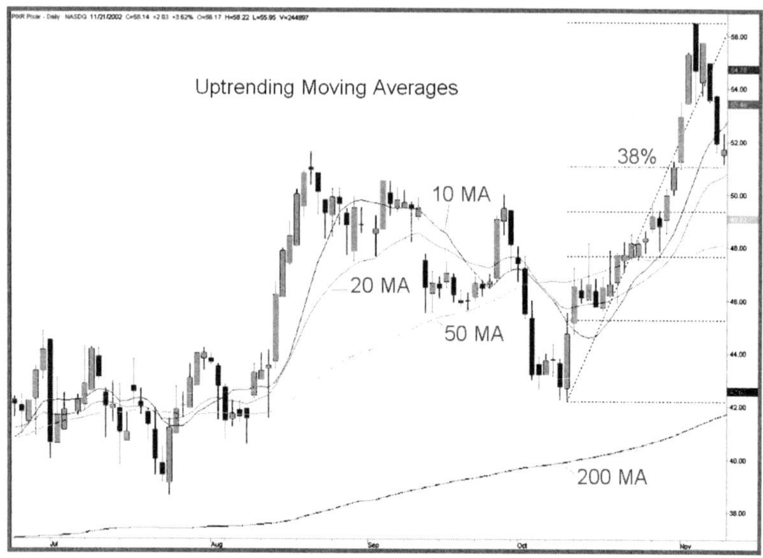

The 200-day MA is so far away that it doesn't really matter much in this case, however, notice that all of the shorter term MAs are sloping up, which is additional bullish confirmation.

Finally, a closer examination of the candles is desired. See the following chart.

You may have already noticed that a Narrow Range Bar appears on the chart at the 38.2% Fibonacci retracement level, which indicates range contraction and consolidation. So, a Narrow Range Bar is a signal of a potential price move.

Okay, here's a recap of where we stand.

There is a strong impulse to the upside that resulted in a new momentum high. The first pullback has occurred, which is the most powerful pullback to consider for a trade setup. We have two support indicators, the earlier swing high point and the 38.2% Fibonacci. Plus, we have up-trending short term MAs and a Narrow Range Bar.

All of the indicators are telling us the next move should be to the upside, except for the Narrow Range Bar. The Narrow Range Bar is more of a volatility indicator. It tells us that a potential price move could come soon as volatility expands.

The Trade

While you could go ahead and enter a long position at this point, it would still be a bit assumptive. And, if bad news or some other negative event occurred, the trade could abruptly go against you. So, I prefer a more cautious approach, which is to put in a buy-stop order slightly above the high of the Narrow Range Bar, as shown on the following chart.

If a move breaks the high, a long position would be entered into with a great risk versus reward ratio. Upon entering the trade, a stop-loss order is placed slightly beneath the newly established retracement low, which should be at or near the 38.2% Fibonacci support level. A retest of the prior high is all that we're after on the trade, which becomes the target for taking profits (or even slightly less than the high). As a result, the upside potential is approximately 4.10 in profits while the risk is only 1.35, which is slightly better than a 3:1 favorable risk-reward ratio.

While some traders or analysts prefer a 3:1 risk reward, such a high ratio is not necessary in my opinion, particularly when other analysis and indicators improve your odds. With proper money management and stop-loss orders that limit losses, you only need to come out ahead on average. I frequently enter trades with only a 2:1 or 1.5:1 ratio and still come out ahead.

With some high percentage plays, I will even enter a trade with a 1:1 risk-reward ratio. For example, the first Bull Flag after a strong impulsive upside move is one of the highest probability trades you can make. Since it's such a high percentage play, I will often enter the trade even if the risk-reward ratio is only 1:1.

On the preceding trade, as with the first example, you would take profits on your entire position when the target price is reached. Or, if you think there is more upside potential, you could sell one-half of your position and move your stop-loss order to breakeven or better on your remaining shares. Afterwards, you would trail any additional upside moves with your stop-loss order until the price reverses and you are stopped out of your remaining shares.

You've reached the end of the examples. Now, it's your turn! Try to do some of your own analysis. If you are just starting out or don't want to risk your capital initially, practice by paper trading until you gain more experience and confidence with technical analysis. You can do your analysis then simulate trades by writing them down on paper (your lot sizes, entry prices, exit prices, times, dates, balances, etc.). Afterwards, watch the outcome and learn from it. Many brokerage firms let you trade in a demonstration mode. You can use the demo mode to simulate trade executions without putting your capital at risk. In time, you will be able to determine what approach works best for you. Then when you are ready, you can test your skill in the market with real trades.